From Forum to Futures

From Forum To Futures

A chronicle of 2,000 years of Britain's commodity markets

David Courtney

© David Courtney
All rights reserved. The contents of this book, either in whole or in part, may not be reproduced, stored in a data retrieval system, or transmitted, in any form whatsoever or by any means, electronic, mechanical, photocopying, recording or otherwise, without written permission.

First published in 1991 by Futures and Options World in Association with Credit Lyonnais Rouse Limited
This edition published by
Hindsight Books Limited 2004

ISBN 0-9541567-3-0

Printed in Hong Kong by
Colour Max Commercial Printing Company Limited

Contents

	Introduction	vii
1	Ancient origins	1
2	The Dark Ages	13
3	The Middle Ages	26
4	The Renaissance and the winds of change	49
5	The rise of free market economics	65
6	Forward into futures	80
	Epilogue	102
	Bibliography	105
	Index	106

Trade is the Wealth of the World;
Trade makes the difference between one Nation and another;
Trade nourishes Industry, Industry begets Trade;
Trade dipenses the Natural Wealth, which Nature knew nothing of.

Daniel Defoe 1728

Introduction

I had never considered that I would someday become involved in the commodity markets, but it happened. Upon the announcement of this major career move, many of my friends and family replied 'Marvellous, aren't they a part of the Stock Exchange or something?' No doubt in my naivety I replied in the affirmative, but was nevertheless eager to get on with the job and to learn the tools of my chosen trade. To my astonishment, I found there was far more to the process of buying and selling commodities than first met the eye. Indeed, the intricacies of the commodities and their related futures markets stimulated a kind of curiosity in me, which I wanted to satisfy. Some time later, by accident, perhaps more than merit, I agreed to write a book on some of the basics of trading commodities and published 'An Investor's Guide to the Commodity Futures Markets' to help those first approaching these markets to answer questions about many of the rudiments involved. It was whilst I was compiling the chapter outlining a brief history of the commodity markets that I discovered a complete lack of specialist material on the subject. I decided at that point that I would attempt to reply to my continuing curiosity and, perhaps, fill a literary void in the process.

To my surprise and delight, I found references to markets and their practices peppered in an astonishing variety of history books. Political, economic, social, architectural and religious works each contained references to markets and their practices. It was not long therefore, before I began to realise just how important commodity markets were.

What follows in this book is, in effect, a condensation of all the various references in chronological order. It does not attempt to analyse the preponderance of the trade in commodities themselves; rather, it attempts to explain how the markets have responded to myriad influences and developed into the markets we recognise today. In so doing I found it quite astounding how complex, yet simple, they are. But perhaps the real strength and the reason for the continued existence of commodity markets, apart from their extreme efficiency, is their ability to adapt. Markets, through the direction of experienced and wise practitioners, have undergone remarkable transformations. They have, in the space of two thousand years, developed from local community trysts into regional fora; national, centralised exchanges; and have matured into international, if not global, affairs.

Introduction

At much the same time, their practices have come a long way from the barter and exchange system prevalent in their early days. For over the same period of time, commodity markets have evolved through forwards, auctions, options, swaps and futures into markets of extraordinary depth and variety.

I hope that now, asked the same question 'aren't commodity markets a part of the Stock Exchange?' I will not be quite as naive in my reply. For I have discovered many things about commodity markets. And one thing is certain: without the commodity markets we would not have a need for a Stock Market. For in turn, much of the commercial fabric of Britain was woven with the threads from the commodity trades. And so this is true, in large part at least, with regard to the banking and insurance institutions we recognise today. In many ways, therefore, the commodity markets are 'the grand old men' of commerce. So it is my hope that this book will encourage the respect for the commodity markets which they so richly deserve.

The author wishes to acknowledge the contributions and assistance of the many people who have made this book possible. Among those who justly deserve special mention are Dr Alan Bowman of Christchurch College, Oxford; and Mr James Bolton of Queen Mary College, London, who each provided many suggestions and shared their experience and expertise. However, certain interpretations of facts expressed within the text do not necessarily correspond identically to those of the afore-mentioned.

A measure of considerable indebtedness is furthermore due to The Tea Council Ltd and The Liverpool Cotton Association Ltd.

Lastly, the author wishes to thank his wife, Sally, and his family for their unending support and encouragement.

DCC

CHAPTER ONE

Ancient Origins

Markets have existed as long as there has been a desire or need to exchange or trade commodities, irrespective of whether the population concerned was contained within a particular community, region, or country or dispersed internationally, and Britain is by no means exceptional. Indeed, for several millennia, the market place has symbolised commerce and prosperity, occupying an unrivalled position at the very heart of almost every community.

In ancient Britain, markets were in existence prior to the Roman invasion in AD 43 and were established as meeting places at which the exchange of goods took place, so that commodities found in profusion were replaced with those in scarcity. In so doing, markets created a mechanism by which the effective distribution of commodities was performed in the most efficient manner possible in any given area. In this way, regional inequalities were alleviated and discrepancies and variations in values, which normally accompany such supply and demand fluctuations, were significantly reduced. In very simple terms, exchange and distribution are the primary functions of markets, though there are myriad other functions which are performed inadvertently and these will be explained in detail as we progress.

Before the arrival of the Romans to Britain, markets were conducted rather more informally, were often unregulated and were held on an irregular basis. Their frequency was entirely dependent upon the demands of the community they were designed to serve. They were simple affairs, used as primary outlets for surplus production, where transactions were made by means of a barter and exchange system, and were concerned with a limited variety of basic commodities. Bartering was a time consuming affair. Each party had to determine the value of his counterpart's goods and evaluate these values with the considered value of his own goods. Naturally, each inflated the true value of his own merchandise and discounted that of his counterpart. Invariably, several minutes would elapse before negotiations were concluded, as often as not unsuccessfully, and the exchange of goods was made. The entire process was evidently an extremely cumbrous affair which severely restricted the number of such exchanges. It was also dependent upon the acceptability of the quantity and quality of the various commodities on offer. Notwithstanding the restrictions such a system promoted, barter and exchange sufficed to perform the functions of trade and distribution on such a modest scale, however problematical and inefficient the system may have been.

Markets at this early stage were almost exclusively retail affairs; that is to say, consumers were in direct contact with producers. The effect of introducing buyers directly with sellers served to minimise the distribution chain and ensured, as much as possible, an acceptably fluent movement of goods. In time, markets were fixed on prescribed days, and took place at acknowledged venues which were conveniently located. Often, the confluence of two rivers, or a ford or bridge were used as they were the simplest locations for people to congregate. These were later complemented with events held at the intersection of ridgeways or drovers' roads which were also suitable in this respect. So strategically were these meeting places arranged that in time settlements invariably developed around them and semi-permanent trading entrepots were created. In many ways, therefore, markets were not so much fundamental to a settlement or village, they were in fact the very reason why people decided to congregate, initially to exchange goods, but thereafter to settle, secure in the knowledge that they could sustain their livelihoods.

Markets such as these mushroomed over the years. They remained isolated from one another so far as organisation was concerned, but were linked in terms of operation. The transition from the hundreds of independent markets into a more discernible marketing system took centuries to arrive. Indeed, this organisation can be largely, if not exclusively, attributed to the Romans during their 400-year rule of Britain. In fact, many of the foundations of the marketing system we recognise today can be traced back to this period. The transition from myriad independent markets into a cohesive system was made possible by two major developments. First, the establishment of towns responsible for the government of provinces; and second, the initiation of a more formal network of roads between towns. These two developments brought about several changes in the marketing regime as towns in time tended to concentrate the population in more definitive areas and this served to create a hierarchical chain of markets. Concentration of people also encouraged trade specialisation and a division of labour. As individuals became more reliant upon the skills of others, so too did they become more reliant on the markets which supplied the staple commodities.

In time, increasing population of certain towns permitted markets to concentrate in a particular commodity to serve specific production or local trade specialisation needs. In so doing, it signalled a new breed of market and a significant progress in efficiency. This in turn was made possible as these markets were able to receive regular supplies afforded by the improvements in transport which were taking place. An effective means of transport was and remains a primary component of an efficient distribution chain. But although marked improvements were made during the Roman occupation of Britain, efficiency as we recognise it today was very limited in comparison and the effective distribution of goods needs to be taken in context. For despite the genesis of a formal and comparatively complex road system, it remained largely inadequate to distribute raw materials efficiently over more significant distances.

Even towards the twilight of the Roman occupation, matters had improved little, if at all. Present-day economists have since theorised from the Emperor Diocletian's Edict of Prices around AD 300 that it was unprofitable for merchants to transport grain in excess of fifty miles overland as the price they were able to secure at any one of the provincial markets generally did not justify the additional costs involved. They continued that due to the level of tolls, taxes and other incidental expenses a cargo of wheat weighing 1200 pounds doubled in price if it were transported 300 miles or more. As a comparison, the record concluded that it was less expensive to transport raw materials by sea over the entire length of the empire than it was to transport the identical goods 75 miles overland. Inevitably, this had an effect on the manner of distribution; roads being used for short distances, rivers for interregional movement and sea for long distances or wherever possible. This in turn had profound effects both on price fluctuations and the location and importance of markets. Supply difficulties, together with the vagaries of production, meant that prices of basic raw materials such as corn were subject to fluctuations of some 100 per cent over comparatively modest distances and time frames. The effects of such price variances and distribution problems, both potentially severely damaging, were addressed by the Roman State, which intervened in any one of a number of ways, and these will be examined later.

Perhaps the primary economic duty of the state was its responsibility to establish markets in order to create a network sufficiently wide to ensure the free movement of commodities. The network was designed to minimise as far as possible any disadvantages of location while promoting local production specialisation. However, transport limitations prevented the establishment of any single central market. Quite the contrary, for although London had been the capital of Roman government in Britain, its markets effectively served only its comparatively dense population; markets peripheral to London were entirely necessary. Indeed, they were established and promoted quite independently.

During the Roman epoch, markets were organised by the state at venues and frequencies reflecting the requisites of each community they served. Of the utmost importance were the emporia or harbour markets. They were strategically located around the country and were responsible for the collection and distribution of raw materials and commodities on a more widespread basis. Often they reflected multi-national influences as merchants from throughout the Empire congregated at these events. As the Roman presence in Britain grew, so too did the number and size of the emporia, which were employed effectively as wholesale markets where substantial transactions of bulky commodities took place. Accordingly, sale was invariably conducted on a sample and receipt basis whereby cargoes were examined for quality by prospective buyers and verified for quantity by a warehouse receipt. Bargains were then struck according to terms agreed without the physical proximity of the commodities concerned. Title and transfer were carried out at a later stage following a more complete examination of the consignment in question.

The emporium was a generally well organised affair, by far the largest venue at which commodities were traded and similarly more frequent than the markets which relied upon its wholesale activities. Nonetheless, throughout the entire duration of the Roman occupation the absence of a central market or news source meant that not only did information vary from one emporium to another, but so too did commodity prices; often for onerously long periods.

Of lesser importance was the forum, which served as both a meeting place and market place. These fora were frequently commissioned by Emperors who were under constant pressure throughout their provinces to accommodate widespread demand for the staple commodities. The construction of a new forum was in many ways as much a politically motivated exercise as it was an economic measure. Increasing the number of fora not only diluted to some extent the problems associated with poor transport, but it also assured each regional Governor some measure of popularity. In time, more or less every regional town boasting some importance or another had a forum of some description. Often they were particularly imposing buildings, possibly on two levels, invariably at the very heart of the town. Many accommodated the needs of local production specialisation. Some were arranged according to specific commodities set among colonnades, whilst others were arranged according to the countries or regions of origin.

As such, the forum was seen to be more of a retail market directly serving the public, where merchants, who had previously acquired inventories from the wholesale emporia, came face to face with consumers. Accordingly, the traders parcelled their stocks of bulky commodities into smaller quantities specifically for individual consumption. The process of buying and selling was therefore far more immediate. Goods were on open display and available for instant inspection, and were able to be taken away upon prompt payment. Fora, by definition, were more numerous than the emporia which supplied them and they in turn served as inter-regional markets organised to attract itinerant traders laden with some of the more exotic or unusual, as well as the staple, commodities. For many, the forum served as the hub of the local economy, where not only commodities, but news and stories were exchanged. In this way, the forum formed the major link with the outside world, which is perhaps why they were so enormously popular.

But not only was the forum a highly popular meeting place, it was also invariably at the centre of municipal institutional town planning. For around them were built the Law Courts, government offices and many other municipal buildings whose functions revolved around routine commercial activities. In this respect, the forum took pride of place, and was for many, and for a long time, undisputed as the principal institution of almost every town.

The structure of the Roman marketing system spanned a further dimension, however. The emporia and fora were well organised and sufficiently numerous to ensure regular and reliable movement of raw materials, but they only served relatively localised areas. To ensure an equally plentiful and frequent exchange of commodities into and out of even the most rural of areas, smaller village markets were organised and promoted to eliminate many of the difficulties geographical location created. Small community markets were known as 'Nundinae' - ninth day affairs, but though they were held regularly, they were not held every nine days as their name suggests, but every eight days, as the Romans counted both terminal days. They were bazaar-like affairs, frequented by local farmers and itinerant traders, where an enormous variety of produce changed hands. Where transport proved especially difficult, they were separated by a standard maximum distance of just four or five miles. But to eliminate local competition, which would have reduced efficiency, they were held on different days of the week, in rotation, so that the cogs of exchange turned with the minimum of interference. In this way, distribution efficiency was optimised such that regular supplies of commodities were exchanged at each of the smaller community markets, which in turn were not only linked together, but were also linked inexorably with the wider and more formal marketing system which supported them.

State Involvement

A great source of exchequer revenue accrued from trade and commerce. Thus, if the exchequer was to flourish, it was highly beneficial that the state provided the machinery for exchange and economic growth, and this function was discharged in a number of ways. First and foremost, the marketing system was a state prerogative - in other words, it was the state that organised and built markets. Under no circumstances did it abdicate this responsibility or delegate it to individuals or other institutions. Moreover, it guarded this duty very carefully; if for no other reason than to safeguard the revenues accruing from market activity. But this was not the only reason. Markets were and remain the most efficient organisations both to regulate and promote trade. For markets not only responded to existing commercial demands, but new markets of new commodities fostered new trades and therefore promoted prosperity and economic growth. Additionally, the concentration of activity at a prescribed place made regulation of activities and protection of patrons a far more simple affair. Without the elements of regulation and protection, any amount of promotion would have been worthless. For both buyers and sellers demanded not only fair price and freedom of choice, but also assurances that their interests were being well looked after.

To ensure that market regulations were observed, the state appointed market policemen who were present to settle any petty disputes, but who also had authority to refer more serious offences to the courts. Disputes arose infrequently in the normal course of business, so it was essential that specific legal courses supported by legislation were available. However, though this was also a responsibility of the state, settling disputes was out of the jurisdiction of the market authorities. They were present to police activities and refer cases to other specialist authorities.

Apart from overseeing trade, the market officials performed other, additional duties. First, with the availability of municipal funds they were able to buy staple commodities during times when supply was plentiful and prices were low. Their acquisitions were then stockpiled until such times as supply evaporated and prices rose, at which time they were empowered to release stocks on to the open market.

Ancient Origins

This was not directly a speculative activity, though profits accruing to such enterprises certainly served to swell the local treasury. It was designed, moreover, to regulate supply and demand oscillations in order to stem wide fluctuations in price. This activity was quite necessary. For apart from the interference of the state in this way, no system existed to mitigate price-changes and the risks which merchants, wholesalers and producers naturally encountered. Though the state forcibly subordinated the interests of the aforementioned to those of the public, it was seen as a necessary and desirable activity in which the state could indulge in order to pursue its responsibilities. Upon occasion where such intervention proved inadequate, market officials also provided price guarantees, a form of subsidy, when prices were at unprofitably low levels and supplies were interrupted. Contrariwise, they were able to introduce and impose rations when supply difficulties were manifest.

On a more routine note, however, market officials were charged with the task of both setting and collecting tolls and taxes. In this regard markets were again considered highly efficient. Not only could the state easily promote, regulate and protect the various interests at heart, but aided by the concentration of people and activity it could also effectively collect the various dues quite simply. In almost every respect markets performed the economic, political, commercial and social tasks with consummate and unrivalled ease. It is, therefore, not surprising that their success has lasted to this day.

The Romans also indirectly encouraged and promoted the commodity trade through the introduction of coinage. Prior to the arrival of the Romans, trading, as we have seen, was carried out on a barter and exchange basis. Coinage, however, eliminated many of the problems associated with barter and exchange. Specifically, it dissolved difficulties relating to acceptability of others' goods and in so doing created a medium by which all values were judged and transactions undertaken. Coinage therefore made the entire process of exchange a far more simple task, which indirectly increased trading activity. Interestingly, coinage betrays its origins in barter. Indeed, for centuries prior to its introduction, cattle, the economic foundation of Rome, were used as a standard, albeit notional medium of exchange. When coins were introduced to replace cattle in the exchange function the Romans referred to the metal ingots as 'pecunia' which derived its meaning from the Latin word for cattle - pecus. So although the transition from barter to coinage appears as an abrupt move, it was far more smooth in reality, having taken place over a number of years before eventually coinage developed a value of its own.

Market Regulations

Regulating markets was a natural extension of state responsibility towards the effective promotion of trade and the protection of its participants. By ensuring fair and honest dealings the state was able to encourage widespread patronage which was not only beneficial for the distribution process, but it also increased revenues from tolls and taxes. Therefore, efficient regulation was desirable for all who were involved. However, it was important not to over-regulate to the extent that practices became overly restrictive. The balance was and remains to this day a difficult one to achieve.

Nonetheless, market officials were present to ensure that certain fundamental rules were observed. First, they ensured that only pure and unadulterated goods were open for sale and that sub-standard or impure commodities were withdrawn. They also monitored prices and fined traders who attempted to make greater profits by altering prices in the wake of different customers. The practice of bringing other traders' business into disrepute was also taken very seriously and fines were also imposed for such unethical practices. But whereas much regulation was imposed upon the merchants themselves, consumers also had certain responsibilities. Payment had to be made punctually upon delivery - any delay was intolerable. In this way, merchants were required to observe the rules and regulations imposed by the state, but in return they were supported and protected against any default on the part of their customers.

Naturally, protection only existed where officials were present and any clandestine trading was not only outside the state's jurisdiction, but those who engaged in this trade were punished severely. Upon the proviso that trade took place at official venues, the presence of market officials served to minimise the number of disputes and through negotiation or threat, the severity of those disputes which arose was mitigated. But even the most efficient policing did not eliminate disputes and a higher legal authority had to be involved. Therefore, all pursuant actions were heard in court within one month, often much less, with a jury reviewing the evidence and delivering the verdict. In this way, disputes were resolved with the least delay, cost and inconvenience: a system which itself protected and promoted the interests of all concerned. As a precaution, merchants involved in large-scale transactions were obliged to remain within the district where the market was located for several days. Accordingly, complete and thorough inspection was carried out before the vendor left to do business elsewhere. It is therefore evident that the Romans recognised prevention was better than cure on matters relating to market regulation. Indeed, these regulations developed over many years and in so doing created a firm foundation for mercantile development.

Weights and Measures

Regulation and promotion was apparent in many forms. One component of this was the state's attempts to impose quantitative as well as qualitative control over commodities on sale at markets. Quality inspections were carried out routinely by the market officials, but although no quality standard was laid down, there were general guidelines as to precisely what was and was not acceptable. More pressing, however, was the need to establish quantitative standardisation. For without the use of weights and measures it was impossible for consumers to compare accurately the cost of any given commodity offered by several merchants. Accordingly, the Romans sought to establish and impose standards of weight and measurement, and both weights and vessels for capacity became a normal part of every merchant's paraphernalia. All those who wished to practise at market were obliged to present themselves to the market officials before the market commenced in order that the weights and measures be verified.

But although the principle was sound, it was somewhat less successful in operation. For the Roman Empire was vast, and standards varied from one market to another. Even in Britain several standard measures existed, so much of the advantages were lost. True, on a local, consumer scale, which was the primary reason behind Standardisation, the use of such weights and measures fostered greater equitability, but on a more widespread basis it was ineffective. Merchants, on the other hand, who practised at several markets, were compelled to carry several different 'standards' which appeared to them to be nothing more than a nuisance. Standardisation was theoretically of great advantage, but to be effective it needed to be more universal. However, despite attempts by the Romans to consolidate the variety of standards it was never able to impose single, uniform weights and measures. Indeed, uniform standardisation was not a condition to be seen in Britain until fifteen hundred years later.

The Black Market

Towards the end of the Roman Empire, and at a time when the Roman Treasury was becoming increasingly depleted, coinage was debased in order to consolidate reserves of gold and silver. This move was met with widespread disapproval and suspicion which led to a state of rapidly increasing inflation.

In response, Roman subjects and citizens attempted to recover the lost value of the coinage by increasing the cost of commodities and other goods pro rata. This act was officially denounced amid protests from consumers that such price increases were intolerable. The state was forced to intervene through every possible means and it decided to impose strict tariffs on myriad goods and commodities at markets, supported by severe punishment for those who chose not to observe the tariffs. The imposition of tariffs inflamed an already tense market situation. It led to the gradual abandonment by many merchants of the state-regulated markets, where tariffs were enforceable. Instead, they congregated in the shadows where officials were absent and where free-market forces prevailed. The increasing absence of merchants at official markets rendered supply difficulties ever more acute - a move which in itself forced prices upwards.

Word of the 'black market' spread. Consumers, faced with higher prices and a shortage of supply, began to boycott the official markets in increasing numbers and frequented the unofficial markets which sprang up everywhere. They forewent the security of regulated, official markets, where prices were high and supply was inadequate, in favour of the black markets which were able to supply almost every need, but under free-market conditions. The compensation for so doing, apart from the security of supply, was the absence of taxes which in itself offset much of the burden of higher retail prices prevailing on the black market.

The state naturally outlawed all such clandestine activity. It imposed heavy fines and imprisonment on offenders, and furthermore, it repealed the merchants' licences and confiscated all the commodities concerned. The risks for both merchants and consumers were therefore acute, but the assurance of provisions and the absence of taxes largely compensated for the risks involved. Neither the merchants nor the consumers complained of the black market. Indeed, many saw it as a natural manifestation of the state's growing incompetence in economic management. Despite attempts to prevent such gatherings, the state was powerless to put an end to the ubiquitous black market. Only when coinage was returned to its previous purity were the inflationary pressures alleviated. But by then the seeds of distrust were sown and the Empire was beginning to decay.

So, the Romans, in Britain and elsewhere, realised at an early stage that markets may well be used to encourage and promote trade and protect the various interests at heart. But over-regulation and enforcement would not be tolerated. Moreover, over-zealous regulation was widely interpreted as a harmful form of interference.

Ancient Origins

Contracts of Deferred Delivery

Although the State's involvement in market activity to mitigate supply and, therefore, price fluctuations did much to arrest the risks involved in the commodity trades, its dwindling reserves during the 2nd century AD demanded that taxation, both direct and indirect, be increased. This placed enormous strains on many or all of its subjects including the producers and farmers of many of the staple commodities. As a consequence, contracts of deferred or forward delivery were established and were used increasingly. Farmers and producers, having sold their crops in advance of harvest, were thus able to meet increasing tax liabilities. These forward contracts were binding as to price and quantity and were finalised upon harvest. There was a risk that adverse climatic conditions could spoil or reduce the crop, but it was a risk which had to be taken. The problem might have occurred in any event, but at least the problem had been deferred with the discharge of the tax liability.

Contracts of deferred or forward delivery were, however, quite uncommon relative to traditional cash transactions. Certainly they were not in widespread use between the time of their introduction and the collapse of the Roman Empire two centuries later. Still, records of them exist. And the use of forward contracting illustrates a noteworthy change to commodity market and trade practices in response to economic demands. But although such evidence documents forward contracting, it tends to suggest that it was solely for the purpose of meeting tax liabilities. There is little evidence to suggest that it was undertaken in order to avoid risks from volatile price movements.

Forward contracting was tolerated by the state, but was viewed suspiciously. Not always were the arrangements accorded or concluded at market, so it was impossible to ensure the prompt and correct payment of tax. Nonetheless, it was difficult to suppress, and with its preponderance came the speculators.

Speculation

It could be argued that merchants are speculators in a sense, as they take certain risks in the performance of their professions. But the true speculators were unconcerned with either the interests of consumers or the function of distribution. They were motivated solely by their desire to profit from fluctuating prices and used a number of ploys to achieve their ends. Speculari, from which the word speculation is derived, literally means 'to spy out' or 'to observe'. So the original speculators watched for opportunities on mostly localised levels and waited to take their profits.

Undoubtedly, the use of forward contracts described above assisted them in their enterprises, but the speculators were by no means reliant upon them. They were quite content to buy at regular market events and hoard their stock until its value had risen. However, this activity was, not surprisingly, actively discouraged, and the state sought measures to prevent manipulation for purely speculative motives. All stocks in excess of a level prescribed by the state had to be declared to the authorities. Those who failed to do so, or who were suspected of hoarding, were committed to trial and, if the allegations were proven, fines, confiscation and imprisonment ensued.

Speculation of this nature is but one example of the changes taking place at the time. But the advent of speculators (and for that matter that of the black market and forward contracting) by no means acted as catalysts of the economic decay and subsequent social disruption which befell the entire Roman Empire. They were, rather, symptoms of it. Notwithstanding this, during the four hundred years of Roman domination of Britain many developments and much progress had been achieved, not least in respect to trade and market organisation. But the extent of the prevailing political and economic problems was beyond repair. Soon the entire fabric of Roman culture was lost and with it came the end of a political and economic miracle.

CHAPTER TWO

The Dark Ages

The disintegration of the Roman Empire in AD 476 came after 400 years of prosperity. It was followed by a period of protracted deterioration which we recognise today as the Dark Ages. When the Romans abandoned Britain's shores, they left in their wake social and political turbulence of unprecedented severity. Disease and conflicts between provincial dictators disrupted the life style of almost every individual. Rural areas saw production of the staple commodities interrupted which in turn encouraged many people to leave the towns created by the Romans in favour of the open country. In so doing, many individuals resorted to subsistence economies, relying upon their own efforts to produce the staple commodities necessary for a basic existence. As a consequence, surplus production was minimised and both trade and produce specialisation were largely eliminated. The arrival of the Dark Ages was thus accompanied by profound social and political change, which also had a dramatic effect on the nature and degree of commodity trade. This in turn indexed a regression in commercial activity which lasted for several centuries.

Another development which contributed to this reduced volume of trade was the ruinous state of the overwhelming majority of roads which were so meticulously constructed throughout the Roman domination into a network of commendable, but limited, efficiency. All but the most important of roads built under the Pax Romana were left to decay into utterly impassable tracks barely adequate for individuals to negotiate, much less those who attempted to use them to ply their trades. Thus, the very arteries and veins of commerce so richly encouraged by the Romans ceased, causing the suffocation of many prospering communities and their markets. The combination of political and governmental upheaval, a changing demographic profile, together with a redistribution of population and an ailing transportation network brought the great Roman marketing system to a painful and sudden halt. Nonetheless, aspects of this highly effective marketing regime were retained, albeit on a much reduced scale and the organisation of markets once again reflected the economic conditions which had befallen the times.

After centuries of suppression, the more cogent local landlords were emerging and were themselves later still subordinated to the Realm. Their appearance and particularly that of the Realm brought about more widespread peace, which in so doing gradually promoted the return to a more commercially orientated way of life. This, in turn, brought markets to the forefront of trade activity once more. Alfred the Great did much to re-establish the market based economy lost for centuries, encouraging more domestic trade as well as securing and developing wider trade routes beyond the shores of Britain. Markets began to attract buyers and sellers in greater numbers despite the general level of poverty created by the austerity of many years of subsistence economy for many at the time.

Nonetheless, a more discernible market system was becoming evident. In general terms, the Anglo-Saxons did much to restore commercial activity and were largely responsible for re-establishing old markets which had vanished along with the Romans; in fact a number of markets today can trace their roots back to this period. Indeed, specific pieces of land attributed to markets in Anglo-Saxon times are still recognisable as such. For instance, a market which specialised in livestock was known as a 'toom' and references have persisted to the present day. An example of this is an area in the centre of Norwich known as Tombland.

The benefits and rewards of an organised market regime were recognised as a foundation to a prosperous nation and the Anglo-Saxons did their utmost to promote such a system. Indeed, by the time of the Norman conquest in 1066, an efficient market system was evident and provided, as will be described later, the basis upon which the Normans, under the Plantagenets, elaborated to re-create a network of markets throughout England which had all but recaptured the system lost on the fall of Rome.

The Extent of Commodity Trade

The volume of trade was already in decline towards the end of the Roman Empire, but the rate of this decline accelerated over the final years. When the Roman Empire eventually fell, trade contracted still further. The absence of a stable government served to further inhibit trade and naturally this undermined the very existence of the commodity markets which had for centuries prospered and expanded. Towns were already being evacuated by an increasing proportion of the population over the final years of Roman government; and this increased as many were no longer assured of the surplus production of others for their existence. Slowly, Britain, like much of Western Europe, witnessed a re-emergence of agricultural communities which strove towards self-sufficiency and the security of the rewards for one's own efforts. Trade thus became an auxiliary function. It was conducted only when extraordinary surpluses of basic commodities were available and effected between the peasant landowners.

With this contraction in commercial activity came the temporary return to barter and exchange which restored a means of trade not seen for several centuries. At this stage trade had been reduced to all but a local activity and this directly contributed to the diminished number of markets where such trade took place. Paradoxically, it wasn't the small, community markets which suffered most; indeed, they were to be the only remnants of the Roman marketing system to survive. Instead, it was the great harbour markets, the emporia, and the regional fora which disappeared in great measure. As the wholesale trade, fostered by the division of labour, declined as more and more people took to the soil themselves, so too did the market places, which were devoted to the wholesale trade, decline. Accordingly for some time after the fall of Rome trade was to remain inadequate to maintain all but the simplest of marketing systems.

Inter-regional trade was widely inhibited by the predominance of conflict between local lords. Indeed, the existence of such trade had all but completely vanished during the most part of three hundred years. Only a few petty traders and pedlars accepted the dangers and difficulties of moving from one area to another to carry out their trade, but even then, it was carried out over comparatively localised areas. The extent of this trade was also severely restricted by the general poverty of the peasant landowners and what little in the way of trade that did take place serviced only the most basic of needs which were unsatisfied on a domestic level.

Meanwhile, some international trade was retained, but it was governed by licence. It was inhibited by the distribution of wealth which excluded all except the lords of the manors and wealthier landowners, such as the Church. But even then, supplies were sporadic and uncertain due, not least, to the exploits of numerous brigands, highwaymen and roughnecks, who patrolled roads and intercepted the traders and merchants who travelled upon them. In response, merchants, for their own protection, travelled by caravan for much of the time. But by any standards, the volume was of meagre proportions and a poor reflection of that which had existed during the Roman occupation. It comes, therefore, as little surprise that such major changes in local, regional and international trade were accompanied by equally far reaching consequences to the marketing of commodities; changes which continued for quite some time.

The Justification for Markets

From the examination of commodity trade volume from the outset of the Dark Ages, it is not unreasonable to question the valid existence of markets which serviced the requirements of principally independent communities. After all, if the functions of distribution and exchange could have been efficiently performed without the need of having to undergo the trouble of organising markets, the reasons behind their utility must become somewhat doubtful. That markets were maintained during this troubled period as instruments of trade is common knowledge, but the motives behind their consolidation are perhaps rather more nebulous. For although the primary motive was the reduction of supply inequalities at every social level, there were ostensibly four separate elements which contributed to their continuation.

First, according to early Anglo-Saxon law, witnesses were required for each and every commercial transaction. This was largely the result of attempts to restrict the freedom of movement of stolen or plundered goods. The notion being that bystanders may either recognise stolen produce or, alternatively provide evidence in the event of future dispute over title. To this end, secret or clandestine transactions were prohibited and 'public arenas' of some description were indispensable. Evidently, testifiers were an important element of the trade in commodities as markets in time even went so far as to designate 'official witnesses' for all transactions, and contracts valued over 4 pence required no fewer than four independent attestors. The value of markets was thus beyond reproach whilst this law prevailed. It was only in the tenth century that the need for impartial attestation was rescinded under the Law of Athelstan, but markets were already of increasing importance and were by this time the subject of various other statutes which protected their existence.

Second, markets through the extraction of tolls and taxes, had, for a considerable period of time, been a source of quite significant revenue for the Roman treasury, and the landlords upon whose domains trade was conducted were reluctant to relinquish this income. However, had trade been conducted freely and unsupervised, many transactions would have escaped their attentions and the various charges they sought to impose would have become untenable as a consequence. With the organisation of trade through prescribed marketplaces, public participation was concentrated in a single arena whereby volume, and thus revenue, was augmented and in so doing the task of tax and toll collection was greatly relieved.

Third, producers and vendors of agricultural produce and other basic raw materials naturally sought to obtain the highest possible prices for their merchandise. Selling to individuals on a separate transaction basis, however, not only restricted prices as the element of buyer competition was avoided, but it reduced the rate at which pursuant sales were struck. The concentration of people at markets, by contrast, was extremely advantageous to traders as increased demand, relative to stable supply, inevitably increased prices. Vendors were thus able to benefit from the potential of receiving higher prices for their merchandise and from the increased measure of demand which improved immeasurably the efficiency of their trade activity.

Last, markets had long been an intrinsic part of communal life as they were not only the centre for commercial practices, but they were often at the heart of social intercourse. Accordingly, they became embedded into urban and rural ordonnance and entrenched into the lifestyles of their dwellers As ubiquitous, commercial institutions, markets were inviolable.

The Importance of Local Markets

The early years of the Dark Ages witnessed a period of profound regression in commodity trade which inevitably influenced the frequency and size of markets and the complexion of the commodity marketing system. The prevailing social unrest and disturbance inhibited the great majority of international trade throughout Britain and much of western Europe. Naturally, the much reduced level of trade pervaded the marketing system. Consequently, it was subjected to the abandonment of all but the most important and well protected emporia markets, which had for centuries before facilitated a relatively efficient and consistent movement of sea borne commodity traffic.

Conflict among landlords contributed to a greater acuteness of market and trade restraint. Peasants under the protection of combative lords were discouraged from trading with one another as neither safety nor security could be ensured. Whereas on the other hand, financial and economic sanctions were valuable instruments in the subjugation of less wealthy adversaries. Unavoidably, it was the peasant masses who suffered most as the propensity to trade with more distant areas, and the reluctance of itinerant merchants to assume many of the related risks created, for many, a state of enforced isolation. Economic severance and independence demanded the complete exploitation of available resources and marginal, and often wholly unsuitable land previously held fallow or marshy was employed to the extreme.

Irrespective of location, the formation of self-sufficient communities was mushrooming and the primary function of exchange was almost uniquely performed through village markets. Virtually starved of the facility of interregional trade and, more importantly, the benefits of effective international trade activity, the rural markets were crucial to each community. Without them, no matter how infrequent or unorganised, the entire mechanism would have ceased. Consolidated as they were, they provided the foundation from which re-development, however implausible at the time, was able to recommence and a basis which was both operative and fosterable. Throughout Britain, these innumerable local markets were the only aspect of the Roman commodity marketing system to be preserved.

Market Constitution

The right to hold a market was not an autonomous decision taken by peasant landowners who looked to dispose of their surplus production; moreover, their organisation was subject to a higher authority possessing jurisdiction over such matters. As markets were essential to commercial activity, permission from local landlords was a significant privilege, and one which reciprocally embodied rights to the collection of taxes and tolls. During the early part of the Dark Ages these charters originated for the most part from one of two sources: the provincial landlords themselves and the Church (see below), both of whom possessed considerable authority and domain.

The granting of markets did not, however, remain an exclusive privilege to the landlords or the Church. As the social order settled and a more stable political environment was fostered, changes to the provision of market charters took place. Towards the close of the Dark Ages the emergence of a more powerful authority created a similarly advantageous commercial climate. The Crown of England in its infancy slowly but progressively altered the way in which markets were held. Both Charles the Bold and Alfred the Great did much to re-establish the commercial fabric of England, together with its marketing system. Principal to this approach was the creation of a system whereby the Crown was the source of market concessions whether they were weekly, annual or specialist in some way. Indeed, it was during the ninth century that Charles the Bold first proclaimed markets were to be made the subject of Royal Charter. Henceforth, charters were granted to various communities upon the condition that the pertinent tolls and taxes were made freely and wholly available to governors appointed by the Crown. These governors were responsible for the collection of all such levies, equitable regulation, and in return, they were remunerated according to the amount of revenue received. Seen in this light, it is evident that the Crown did not discharge its responsibilities towards markets; moreover, it delegated the duties to reliable and trustworthy officials who carried out the matters concerned. Fraudulent activity or incompetent organisation did not see the foreclosure of the concession, but a replacement of the market governor. In this way, the Crown assumed progressively more control of proceedings.

However, taken as a barometer of general trade activity at this stage, markets were somewhat irregularly and intermittently held, due to annual cycles of the agricultural year. Indeed, by definition, many would be more accurately described as marts rather than markets. For whereas markets suggest elements of regularity and frequency, marts were quite the opposite, convened upon occasions when either excessive supply or demand dictated. Irrespective of their precise form, they were equally well disposed to satisfy the economic tasks at hand, and conformed with political, legal and social criteria. The efforts of the Crown, particularly Alfred the Great, ensured recovery from the depths of the Dark Ages, such that when William the Conqueror successfully invaded England in 1066 a comparatively complex system was present and undergoing further development.

For much of the Dark Ages, however, dominial fragmentation and independence prevented uniformity of either organisation or development as each market was responsive to idiosyncratic local demands. It was only with the emergence of the Crown that uniformity began to appear, although even then widespread differences were apparent. Nevertheless, the markets' elementary functions were consistent throughout the period. Contrasting with the broad range of commodities and finished products characteristic of their Roman counterparts, they remained invaluable for:

i) the supply and distribution of foodstuffs, which was unquestionably their principal objective, and
ii) the supply and distribution of secondary raw materials necessary for small scale, agriculturally inclined industries, though admittedly, this was very much a subordinate pursuit.

The quota of markets during the early part of the Dark Ages was, however, by no means prolific. Population had diminished considerably in comparison to the Roman epoch and communities were comparatively widely dispersed and few in number. Such was the prolonged state of social unrest and commercial stagnation that the number of markets altered very little over several centuries. It was not until the successful institution of the Crown and the restoration of order of some measure that this situation was improved and new markets began to emerge. For stability provided a great stimulus to trade. Gradually the peasant masses were encouraged to forfeit their land in favour of limited employment opportunities in more urban areas. Trade began to re-emerge as the division of labour demanded exchange. Wider trade activity created greater monetary circulation and markets proliferated with the expansion of urbanisation and population.

Churches and Monasteries as Marketplaces

Even in antiquity, religion and trade were linked. As far back as Ancient Greece, temples of gods who patronised various aspects of routine life were employed as exchanges of many of the staple commodities. Temples were perfectly natural locations for traders and consumers to meet. As divine institutions, they were held as places of worship; worship that harvests were plentiful. Not unnaturally, grace was given to the god of each agricultural discipline at the appropriate temple which developed such that exchange of the commodities concerned became a natural extension of the ritual of worship, thereby inadvertently creating an informal ancient exchange system. Rome perpetuated this link and even embellished it over time. Numerous temples were erected and in more urban areas they were concentrated around a particular district or area. In Rome for example, the Aventine Hill was noted for the variety of pursuits these temples sponsored. Evidently, this was much endorsed by the civic authorities who organised living quarters in the vicinity for itinerant traders to encourage more widespread patronage.

For their part, members of the clergy received donations from the traders to secure the kind fortune bestowed by their patron gods. This was effected on a voluntary basis and varied from individual to individual. Nonetheless, these donations were invariably sold and the proceeds distributed either to improve existing temples or construct others throughout the Empire. In this way, an informal, religiously sponsored network of exchanges was created, thus improving the means of distribution to all but the most remote of areas. However, though temples were invariably used as exchanges, trade was by no means the principal reason for their existence. While they were perfectly adequate to perform some of these duties they were never consciously contrived for the activity.

As needs became more complex in response to a larger and more complex society, temples were not developed to meet these needs. The theme of temple exchanges was therefore phased out over a period of time as markets became sufficiently well located and organised to replace them.

Following the dissolution of the Roman Empire many temples were destroyed and abandoned, but the link between religion and commodity markets remained. Holy men had long taught the world that God was responsible for the provision of food and materials for shelter, and certainly the troubled times of the Dark Ages were not exceptional. If anything, the bond strengthened in the face of bitter austerity. Indeed, there is much evidence to suggest that markets at this time were equally religious affairs as they were mercantile, and without doubt significant market evolution can be attributed to Church support and protection of trade. The reasons why and how this was achieved are essentially threefold.

First, considerable land had fallen under Church control, with bishops presiding over provinces which embraced as many as 25 or 30 villages and smaller hamlets. As both outright landowners and lords over numerous peasant tenants, the Church had significant quantities of surplus agricultural produce and required means for their disposal.

Second, the Church was notionally independent of and politically neutral to the influence of the landlords. But although examples of a less than neutral stance have been documented, generally speaking the Church's reported indifference to political motives and its wider presence created unique and comparatively universal commercial and social foundations.

Lastly, the Church was under a moral obligation to provide the staple commodities for the pious, but despite its reluctance to distribute its produce free of charge, it was able to demonstrate its position as purveyor if it were apparent that the Church was responsible for the diffusion of the basic raw materials, albeit indirectly.

In summary, the Church was economically, politically and socially in an impregnable position to provide and organise markets for the pandemic good.

Churchyards, and later areas adjacent to cathedrals, frequently acted as marketplaces, where local produce was sold under the direction of the bishop or abbot. Traditionally, market day was the Sabbath as the pious were released from routine activities and were thus at liberty to attend. Commonly, they commenced in the early afternoon following the morning service and concluded at dusk prior to evensong. In this way, the interaction between religion and commerce is nowhere better illustrated and the market cross became the ubiquitous hallmark of commercial prosperity. Church markets, furthermore, enjoyed an unrivalled popularity and became almost sacrosanct as patrons were protected even from arrest for unconnected offences upon the proviso that they did not breach the peace.

Monasteries, however, differed from the Church insofar as they constituted independent orders, albeit with comparatively consistent practices. They too possessed land and privilege, which provided not only valuable commodities, but rights to hold markets within the confines of their walls. Their wares attracted increasingly wider audiences and progressively distant export markets were secured. Indeed, monasteries were largely responsible for what little interregional trade existed at the time.

Market Regulation and External Influences

The predominance of economic isolation and the absence of interdominal intercourse early in this period not only prevented uniform market development, but they also created dichotomies in the manner in which they were policed. Initially, they were regulated by their organisers, although in fairness, the landlords were comparatively unconcerned with disputes; providing their financial interests were not infringed they accepted little responsibility to solve the polemics which arose. However, those cases which were referred to them were discharged with little legal foundation. Based upon the doctrine that God was the ultimate judge of all men's actions, trials were originally effected either by battle or by ordeal. The notion being that the surviving party was protected by God's grace and he must, therefore, have been the innocent party.

Obviously, this was an ineffective method of dispute resolution, and certainly a dubious foundation for mercantile jurisprudence. As a result, this overtly inadequate legislation between traders was replaced by codes of conduct and customs of general practice agreements. They reflected the consensus of opinion and developed quite independently of the demands of the activity they administered. The customary laws which evolved between traders were tantamount to self-regulation inaugurated to provide basic systematised procedures in circumstances whereby little reliance could be placed on equitable higher jurisdiction. Accordingly, traders and merchants not only formulated market regulations, but by the ninth century they were already engaged in routine police and prosecutional matters without external interference. Disputes were addressed to merchants' courts where the decision of an independent jury was conclusive. For the first time in market history, merchants and traders were an autonomous collective with increasing powers over their own destinies. Indoctrinated from the precedents they set was the renowned Lex Mercatoria.

The preponderance of more stable government during the tenth century supported this approach, but it sought methods to bring self-regulation into more rational context. The autonomy which prevailed continued, but it was subject to a higher legal authority, and the laws of the land were supreme. However, the merchants' influence had become a formidable adversary, for laws in the tenth century prohibiting Sunday markets to protect the Sabbath proved wholly ineffectual. The practice endured for many centuries, and is but one illustration of the control the merchants had promulgated.

The tenth century also saw attempts by the Anglo-Saxon King Edgar to impose uniform and standard weights and measures throughout the kingdom. Notionally, they were designed to replace the various units in use and to arrest the deployment of artificial weights and measures which were in some way deficient. This was indicative of the tide proffered to encourage commercial activity. It was itself the forerunner of the system of assize and later still, the introduction of qualitative as well as quantitative standardisation.

These incidents were certainly the exception rather than the rule for much of the period; it was not until the tenth century when more stable government and the monarchy emerged that more widespread political organisation began to assert greater influence over increasingly flourishing trade and codification of laws was made possible.

Traders and the Need for Itinerancy

Market traders were either local producers of the staple commodities or itinerant merchants, although the former category, certainly in the earliest part of this period, would have constituted by far the greater proportion. However, the extent of movement among peasants was severely restricted by their ultimate landlord. Their ability, therefore, to practise at markets other than those trysts operating at their most immediate village was similarly restrained. The importance of local markets must, therefore, never be overlooked.

What little inter-community or regional trade that did take place was almost entirely in the hands of petty pedlars who, without land of their own, were compelled to trade in order to secure a basic living. Many of the early traders were pilgrims who sought security from the wider presence and non-political motives of the Church. Although this by no means protected them from the ravages of all highwaymen and robbers, they were, as a consequence of their own political objectivity and allegiance to the Church, afforded relatively safe passage through other landlords' domains, upon payment of the customary tolls. For the most part, these pilgrims frequented many of the churchyard markets, thereby supporting the Church's moral obligations of supply, and in so doing, contributed to the wealth of the Church through the payment of the conventional taxes. This again emphasises the role of the Church in the pursuit of trade during the early part of the Dark Ages, and serves to exemplify the relationship between religion and commerce.

Indeed, in some instances, these pilgrim traders relinquished direct interest in trade in favour of acting as commercial agents for the Church in its attempts to sell its surplus commodities. The practice of engaging agents was indispensable for those who were either unwilling or unable to attend markets themselves; and it was one which was echoed by other wealthy landowners later in the period. These 'negotiatores' assumed the trading responsibilities of their patrons and, as their name suggests, they negotiated the best possible commercial arrangements.

Whether they were acting as principals or agents, the traders' nomadic lifestyle was, however, not by any means preferred, but more likely enforced. Firstly, time spent en route was time not spent buying and selling, therefore reducing transactional capacity and the opportunity to profit; and secondly, piracy was both a considerable commercial risk and personal danger. To the traders' detriment, markets and villages were too small and impoverished for them to be adopted as a base of some kind. The infrequency and dispersion of villages, therefore, compelled itinerancy, albeit the practice was against their better judgment and commercial common sense. It was not until the genesis of towns with greater populations that traders could settle to some degree.

Apart from local or regional specialisation, traders were engaged in the trade of a variety of products and, to a great extent, avoided reliance upon any single commodity. Concentration implied and invited risk which could be neither mitigated nor dispensed with, whereas diversification tended to reduce the risks involved. Volume of trade furthermore contributed to the prevention of trading specialisation.

With the degree of commercial revival in the late ninth and tenth centuries, came the tendency of traders to gravitate towards settlements known as wiks. They were initially Viking trading entrepots where merchants obtained local merchandise and were founded and protected by provincial landlords. Thereafter, certain wiks became temporary endroits of residence during the winter months when trade activity dwindled. They were subsequently adopted by itinerant merchants as places of permanent habitation throughout England and Europe, using their clustered houses, set within crude protective barriers, as warehouses and commercial bases. But by this time the wiks were far from exclusive to Viking traders; and were increasingly adopted by merchants of all nationalities. The original wiks have, however, not been forgotten in history. They have, moreover, been incorporated into the names of towns throughout Britain. Even today they may be readily identified, as towns and cities whose names conclude in 'wick', such as Warwick. Similarly, town names ending in 'wich', such as Ipswich and Norwich testify to Viking trading centre origins. With the arrival of such settlements the necessity of extensive travel slowly diminished and with the climax of the first millennium came the establishment of burgs, or towns, which together laid major foundations for commercial evolution over the ensuing centuries.

CHAPTER THREE

The Middle Ages

By the close of the first millennium AD Britain, like much of western Europe, had overcome the many problems of war and austerity and had begun to flourish from the stability afforded by political reorganisation. Population grew dramatically over the ensuing centuries and both welcomed and benefited from a rejuvenation of commercial confidence. First towns, then cities developed from scattered trading settlements. Each one bred arteries of prospering satellite agricultural villages which extended with the preponderance of urban demands. The smaller towns became inexorably linked with their larger neighbours while the advantages of access to ports and wider European markets became increasingly valid in time, and grew to become a prerequisite for mercantile survival. Gradually, various towns and cities established their pre-eminence in the trading hierarchy and emerged as axes for national and international commerce which have been retained to this day.

For the first time in over five centuries, centres of specialisation were able to reappear as individuals relied upon trade to satisfy the absence or scarcity of either the staple commodities or finished manufactured products. New commodities rose in economic prominence, with wool and cloth accounting for a third of the total trade during the thirteenth century. Cotton was more widely used, but was still of secondary importance; sugar was considered an effective and inexpensive replacement for honey and, finally, iron rose to far greater significance in comparison with other base metals in terms of the volumes traded.

The thirteenth century also saw the emphatic regeneration of the eastern trade route following the great Crusades. This secured the restoration of the ancient trade routes which extended to India, China and beyond. A European marketing system embracing Britain was re-inaugurated to facilitate the movement of goods of all descriptions over ever-extending distances, and markets were further consolidated as primary outlets for both commodities and consumer goods. Meanwhile, grain and wool were transported over ever increasing distances to satisfy urban demands. In turn, the growth of towns and their staple requirements demanded considerable improvements in market efficiency and a return, in principle, to the pyramid structured marketing system developed by the Romans. Peripheral professions evolved from the increasing sophistication and progress which the general marketing system realised. By the end of the thirteenth century this had surpassed the degree of complexity of its ancient forerunners in a number of ways.

Transport and its Influence on Markets

In the same way as the Roman marketing system had developed, the establishment and concentration of markets throughout Britain in the Middle Ages was influenced by location, accessibility and most economical mode of traffic. Roads remained largely inadequate for commercial needs and were hazardous even into the twelfth century, although the explosive growth in volume of trade over the period demanded and produced notable improvements. The responsibility was focused upon the Crown and its representatives who, by either assembling important provincial markets, or, alternatively, wishing to establish and promote new markets, were compelled to address the problems resulting from poor overland trade routes. The thirteenth century witnessed the inauguration of a network of roads built to satisfy mercantile requirements. Each new route was accompanied by numerous toll stations, although increasing numbers led to competition between them and fortunately toll rates decreased as a consequence. Nevertheless, when comparing the costs of road transport with river and maritime freight, it is evident that the costs of overland movement of goods still inhibited large-scale distribution of many of the staple commodities.

Efficient sea transport was an obvious requirement for international trade, and markets in towns boasting ports, which had previously been neglected or abandoned, grew in response. Seaborne freight retained its prominence as the easiest and least expensive mode of transport, while rivers were also highly favoured. Towns such as London which were able to benefit from access to both sea and river possessed an obvious advantage; it was an advantage which ensured their development into centres of major international activity.

The expansion of trade facilitated specialisation in every respect and the essential function of movement and distribution of produce was no exception. During the Early Middle Ages guilds (described generally in greater detail later in this chapter) were organised to perform specific tasks in the overall marketing function.

Professional carters increased rapidly in numbers; convoys between rural areas and rivers of closest proximity were becoming ever more commonplace. But the carrying of goods over roads remained an arduous and dangerous occupation. Not to be discouraged, carters transported the staple commodities by packhorse trains of 40 or 50 head. Each one was saddled with wicker panniers full to overflowing, with each head carrying up to 250 pounds of merchandise. Meanwhile, livestock was driven 'on the hoof' by drovers, over increasing distances to towns' markets whose demands were seemingly insatiable. Whether by hoof or by train, merchants were thereby able to dispense with the exhausting and difficult task of transporting their produce themselves, in favour of concentrating their efforts on the more important aspects of buying and selling.

Freight, towards the end of the twelfth century, had already advanced such that consignments of commodities were able to be forwarded in advance of markets, and as speed of foot was greater than the speed of wagon, it meant merchants were able to frequent more markets over the same period of time. Carters continued to grow in number and stature to become a common feature by the close of the Middle Ages, and adopted progressively wider responsibilities. They were legally bound to collect and deliver merchandise to and from market destinations and charged a set fee per mile representing around one and a half per cent of the value of wool and approximately fifteen percent of that of grain. Distributive efficiency was quite clearly greatly improved and with it came the dawn of a new era.

Monarchial Roles and Control

The return of more uniform political order and stability was accompanied by trade supervision, achieved by way of objective, competent and effective royal domination. Economic evolution was a primary objective but, left to the traders and merchants themselves, and subject entirely to free market influences it would plausibly have resulted in damaging, if not potentially disastrous consequences. For the benefit of the nation and, no doubt, their own profit, trade was directed by the Crown, though the role and importance of the merchant guilds was maintained to account for routine commercial matters. Needless to say, mercantile law took precedence over any rules and codes of conduct the traders and merchants devised; and newly introduced laws demanded, upon occasion, changes in these practices.

The principal sovereign role was, theoretically, to safeguard the interests of the Royal subjects and intervene whenever they were contentious and conflicting. Embargoes and enforced trade routes or channels were imposed upon occasion, whilst traders from hostile lands were prevented from attending domestic markets and, later, fairs. Similarly, resident traders were prohibited from practising in foreign markets if war or other political disputes existed between the two countries.

William the Conqueror, following his successful invasion of England in 1066, endeavoured to assume control over both the marketing system and trade in general. The assertion of his authority was directed to protect revenue recovered in the form of tolls, taxes, customs duties and the like; develop uniform legal codes; and furthermore, to improve trading conditions through consistent and objective direction and organisation. Markets thenceforth were conducted purely in those urban or rural locations designated by the Crown. They were subject to royal charter and accompanied by a licence and certain privileges. However, the granting of such a licence was highly advantageous to the holder, who in return paid the King handsomely for the favour; in fact, such was the growth in markets at the time that the granting of market and fair charters contributed a sizeable portion to the nascent Norman exchequer. Accordingly, the king was the principal beneficiary and sole authority over the organisation of the rapidly developing marketing system; a practice which continued for many centuries.

Edward I sought to extend his jurisdiction over international trade by appointing 'staple' ports which were specified and authorised export entrepots where customs officers were empowered to levy and collect revenues (the origin and importance of the English staple system is explained later in this chapter). As the staple ports were few in number the volume of business transacted there increased markedly and the concentration of merchants served to encourage wider patronage. As it coincided with a general surge of demand in tandem with rising population, the staple system became an invaluable instrument in the pursuit of efficiency. For example, this system was greatly responsible for the increase in wool exports from 5,500 tons in 1273 to 8,300 tons in 1305; and a similar pattern prevailed in the trade of tin from Cornwall and lead from the Mendip Hills in Somerset. On the face of it, the staple ports were essential components in the mechanics of Britain's international trade and their inception was a principal part of Royal commercial management. In thirteenth century England, export licences were devised and granted to various noblemen and other influential or prominent individuals as a means of procuring greater revenue. They were available upon application and subscription, incorporating rights to safe passage and 'reasonable' taxes. The major advantage of these licences was the ability to export the staples at venues other than the staple ports. It was, however, a highly discriminatory system which excluded the majority of merchants and was typical of the aberrant policies engineered to satisfy the kings' rather more avaricious motives.

Exports were considered the key to augmenting national wealth and thus occupied a major share of attention. England's kings' preoccupation was long concentrated on increasing their personal wealth. They imposed few sustained commercial policies, preferring to modify their expediences as conditions dictated. Two measures were consistent, however: their encouragement for merchants to expand their activities on the continent, and a subsidy on wool, by far the most important commodity of the time, which was granted to all merchant staplers and those in possession of licences to stimulate the export trade further. As the Crown insisted upon at least partial if not total repatriation in bullion, the exchequer, through the levying of taxation and duties, was in an ideal position to supplement its reserves of precious metals. The innovatory staple system proved to be an unqualified success in virtually every respect.

Sporadic domestic shortages of the paleable grains (i.e. wheat, corn, barley etc.) were, by contrast, very problematical. They could not be solved by the farmers and peasant landowners, whose production was dictated by their own selfish motives rather than moral obligations. However, individual preferences and prejudices could not be seen to subordinate the welfare of the population and it was often appropriate, if market forces proved inadequate, for the Crown to intervene in order to stimulate more widespread production of wheat and barley and occasionally prevent the use of oats for brewing purposes. Although it is unlikely that England's kings could have influenced either landlords or their tenants directly in their production preferences, they were in a position to persuade their subjects through the imposition of taxation. By increasing or decreasing rates according to agricultural activity they were able, at least in part, to encourage or discourage cultivation as necessary.

Evidently, the Crown was beginning to assert greater influence over the conduct of trade and commerce, and in so doing, fashioned rather more uniform and equitable systems to replace their sometimes idiosyncratic and variable antecedents. Inevitably, the tremendous advances in political organisation, together with those in transport, had profound effects on the marketing system. Over the course of the following centuries many of the mercantile elements we recognise today were in their infancy and growing rapidly.

Market Expansion

In contrast to the independent and isolated markets established by the landlords of the Dark Ages, their equivalents during the Middle Ages were instituted by the judiciary, proclaimed by royal charter, perpetuating what Charles the Bold had done in the ninth century, and were beginning to change quite rapidly in character. The Doomsday Book of 1086 mentions just 42 chartered weekly markets in England, although the population explosion during the ensuing centuries demanded significant additions to their ranks. Between the end of the twelfth century and that of the fifteenth, as many as 5,000 royal charters had been granted, over fifty per cent of which were recorded during the first seventy-five years of the thirteenth century.

The rate at which markets were established was not an altogether consistent one. For the mid-fourteenth century witnessed a profound departure from the trends of the twelfth and thirteenth centuries. The Black Death put an abrupt end to the preceding period of expansion. It was responsible for the deaths of millions of people, which both directly and indirectly affected the number of markets in existence. Whereas previously almost every village had a market of some description, the Black Death was responsible for the loss of almost two-thirds, many of which disappeared forever despite attempts to revive them. Despite the vicissitudes of commercial life brought about by natural phenomena, new charters were granted even after the Black Death, but on a much reduced scale. Meanwhile, charters were granted in Scotland by the Scottish monarchy at much the same pace and following a similar trend. But England and Scotland were not alone in this respect. For, albeit that exact chronologies do not exist, the proliferation of markets in Britain was accompanied by that on the Continent and the statistics above are largely indicative of the genesis throughout much of western Europe as well as in Britain.

Whereas certain weekly village markets were considered customary due to the period of their establishment (any existing prior to 1189 were considered to be before legal memory and thus protected by prescription), the Crown insisted upon these charters for strictly economic purposes. Firstly, the considerable income derived from these franchises was renewable upon their expiry as each charter was valid only for a prescribed duration. Second, and of equal importance, was the control over organisation and regulation. Together with the increasing use of standards or assize, these measures ameliorated the efficiency and uniformity of the marketing system, particularly in response to a significant acceleration in demand. Unquestionably, royal control was a major factor in market evolution, and certainly the effects of their involvement became increasingly apparent in time.

But in view of the multiplicity of newly chartered markets, who were the recipients of these formal licences, and where were the markets established? There were two distinct categories applying for the right to hold markets, reflecting quite contrasting motives. The first group was that of the burgesses or guildsmen of the embryonic towns, who were principally concerned with a means of conducting their business and attracting wider audiences to their activities. The Church and wealthy individuals constituted the second category, whose interests were influenced by the investment opportunities markets provided. For whilst each may have had disposable produce themselves, they were primarily concerned with the income derived from the myriad of tolls they imposed upon market participants. Having paid the licence in the customary manner and the fee-farm (a prescribed levy in quittance of all tolls) to the Exchequer, the remainder was entirely profit, and often represented a worthwhile return on the capital outlay. Furthermore, the charter embodied rights to transfer title to the market through either inheritance, or sale subject to enquiry into the prospective purchaser's suitability. In this way, a market could yield not only an attractive income, but potentially create an additional and attractive capital gain.

However, in 1285 the importance of the Church, with its diminishing intercourse with trade, was considerably curtailed as a statute was passed which supposedly heralded the end of the Church markets in England. Theoretically, their licences were rescinded to preserve the honour of the Church and its ministers from the polemics and unbecoming market practices which had evolved. It was, however, perhaps influenced more by political and economic motives in attempts by the Crown to arrest the Church's powers and prestige. It did not, however, prevent the continuation of many Church markets, for despite this precedent they continued for several centuries - well into the sixteenth century, in fact.

The markets' locations were influenced by two elements: geography and accessibility. Random meeting places, through their metamorphosis into wiks, tended to become more permanent domiciles, often, as we have seen, at the point of a river where it was first bridgeable, or at the confluence of two great rivers. The settlements were either incorporated as boroughs on royal demesnes or privately ordained, and emerged from the small urban communities into many present-day towns and cities, with a market place, a central issue to town planning, at their foundation. Even today, evidence of markets long disappeared is manifest in street patterns. An open expanse of land, triangular or wedge shaped, with the main thoroughfare broadening to embrace pens for livestock and storage for other commodities, is often an easily identifiable mark of bygone times.

Throughout England the growth of towns drew supplies of commodities from their environs; and as they grew in size their trading arteries extended and coincided. Unprecedented demand in turn demanded greater sophistication to enable the continuous supply of commodities to the towns, and markets had not so much to increase in number as we have seen, as to become more frequent and more specialised. Most markets were held weekly, but some of the more important events lasted a week or more, even to become semi-permanent features in time.

But such was the proliferation of markets in the thirteenth century that complaints of inordinate numbers abounded and some method had to be devised to restrict further additions. The Plantagenets decided that new markets had to be limited in number and sought a device which they could use to pursue this goal. Thomas Bracton, a noted lawyer, stated that a man could travel a distance of some twenty miles in a day and that an excursion to a market consisted of one third of the day en route for the market, one third at the market, and the remaining third on the return journey. He therefore postulated that the standard radius of a market should be one third of the maximum day's travelling distance or six and two-thirds miles. From these observations the Plantagenets decided the minimum distance between markets was thirteen and one-third miles.

Invariably, market patrons made the journey as much as an outing of adventure as a trade affair, and overnight rests were becoming commonplace. Inns and public houses mushroomed, and were often found in the vicinity of both the market and 'Silver Street' where ladies of the night made the adventure a most congenial affair.

New markets were granted upon the proviso that they did not infringe or injure those already in existence and this was supported by a charter of Edward III in 1327. Excessive numbers of markets unavoidably created competition, and promotion became prerequisite. Tremendous privileges were bestowed upon traders in order to attract participation, but conflict, destruction and embargoes ensued; roads were even blocked to prevent access to competitors' markets. Security became an ever important issue and steps had to be taken to safeguard patrons' persons as well as their merchandise. It became increasingly common for the presiding landlord to assure safety and to despatch guards to patrol approach roads. In time, the glove of the landlord, brandishing his noble coat of arms, became an assurance of safety; invariably a glove was left outside the towns' gates for the duration of the market so as to deter any would-be adversaries.

Threats to personal safety were patently intolerable on a social level, but they were also damaging to market efficiency, and so the problem of over-competition had to be addressed. As markets were held between dawn and dusk in winter and between six a.m. and late afternoon in the summer months, the market hours, signalled by bells to open and close proceedings, could clearly be extended little. Despite the banning of Sunday markets during the tenth century and the reiteration during the thirteenth century, it was little enforced and the Sabbath remained the traditional market day. The first record of attempts to action this law was the thirteenth century chronicle of the Abbot of Burton's application for a market licence. Permission was granted, providing his market was not convened on the Sabbath, Saturday being the preferred day. The precedent it set effectively spread market days throughout the week and the calamitous effects of competition were abated, though they were by no means eliminated. It was not until the full effects of the Black Death had been manifested that the disappearance of many markets finally provided a solution.

Market development was quite consistent, however. By the twelfth century semi-permanent markets trading in all manner of commodities and manufactured goods were prominent in the larger market towns, whereas in others bi-weekly markets were organised to contend with ever-increasing demand. As volumes continued to rise, specialisation in one or a number of closely related commodities became preferable, if not prerequisite. During the thirteenth century some markets nominated specific and separate days for each category of commodity, while other markets allocated segregated areas under separate market crosses for exclusive trading.

Markets were for the most part all-embracing insofar as both commodities and manufactured goods were on sale. This indistinguishability certainly prevailed until the more specialist markets emerged towards the close of the thirteenth century. Irrespective of the goods in question, however, markets were the instruments of all routine and daily trading activity on a local and regional scale. International trade was, by contrast, first accomplished through fairs and later replaced by permanent markets, such as the staple system in England, as volume dictated. Both of these systems are described more precisely below.

The marketing of metals was again rather more idiosyncratic and was not found in direct parallel to other commodities. Metals, moreover, were first formed by rural smelters into the customary ingots or blooms, thereafter taken to locally specified entrepots on prescribed days, where they were weighed, then assayed. Thereafter, they were taken by traders to either the important urban markets whose industrial requirements predominated, or they were transported to the ports for export and wider distribution. Therefore, comparatively little in the way of metals appeared at the rural markets, contrasting markedly with the universality of the agricultural commodities.

International Fairs

A major innovation of the Middle Ages was the great trade fairs which originated from one of three sources. Some had existed since time immemorial and were thus held under the doctrine of 'prescriptive rights' in the same way as markets which were established beyond living memory. Others were religious affairs, often known as wakes, and began as congregations around shrines on saints' days during the ninth and tenth centuries; although in time the religious significance of many tended to be overlooked. As a consequence a number of the early fairs assumed the names of their patron saints. Once again, the Church was the founder and spirit behind their success, although the control and creation of fairs in the eleventh century became a royal prerogative, subsequently established by charter in the same way as markets. Indeed, the major source of franchises for the most part of the period was the Crown. There were, however, fundamental differences between fairs and markets. Notably, fairs were:

i) under higher legal jurisdiction;

ii) not restricted by the province, but were larger and international;

iii) seasonal affairs, not weekly. Most took place in summer and autumn;

iv) given special terms for tolls and taxes, with other benefits for merchants.

In many legal respects, however, there were few differences between markets and fairs until the nineteenth century, when the commercial standing of many fairs disappeared. In the early twentieth century the distinction was finally indited in Halsbury's 'Laws of England'. It stated that 'a market or mart and a fair are each at common law a franchise conferring a right to hold a concourse of buyers and sellers. The terms are, strictly, applicable to the right itself and not the concourse or the place where it assembles. The only distinction between a market and a fair is that the latter is a big market held once or twice a year, whilst the former is something small held once or twice a week.' It was only when the fairs either ceased or conceded their commercial motives and resumed their original religious themes that the distinction became evident.

In operation, however, the fairs allied rural and urban areas with the world at large. They were 'desirous and joyous affairs' held between spring and autumn for various durations, originally two, three or four days, but grew to embrace a week and in isolated cases to several weeks, as population and demand expanded. Some towns even organised several fairs during the season. The local fairs attracted people from nearby towns and villages as they presented the only occasion when they might come into contact with merchants from many nations. They were widely considered to be holidays, often borrowing the term from the holy day they observed, and were greeted as a time of great merriment. Side shows, minstrels, jugglers, music for dancing and a panoply of other diverse attractions were arranged for entertainment. Heavy drinking was endemic and some licensing laws were relaxed to the point where complaints of loutish and rough behaviour threatened the events' very existence.

Notwithstanding this, the popularity of fairs ensured they became gradually more numerous as they proved to be extremely profitable affairs. They were chartered in the same way as markets and thus presented investment opportunities also. As many were initially held to celebrate saints' days which varied from town to town, they were sequential throughout England and Europe, and although they may have been infrequent on a localised level, nationally they spanned several months of the year. As they accumulated in number, competition raged whenever periods conflicted and advantageous tolls were granted to encourage participants.

As a matter of routine, the fairs were opened and closed with great ceremony with the Common Crier leading a procession of bailiffs, coroners, chamberlains and other dignitaries. Trading was again started by the signal of bells, and each fair commenced by proclamation and injunction detailing what was and was not permitted, although this did vary from one to another. Sales were contracted between merchants and consumers on a retail level, and among merchants on a wholesale level from open displays. Stalls were rented from the fair owners and arranged in categories either by the type of merchandise, or by merchant origin. Similar to market practices was the 'open outcry' method of publicising wares and prices which had prevailed since markets began. Certainly the noise level in peak times was almost intolerably high, but this did add to the hustle and bustle of the proceedings. 'Open outcry' survives to this day at many of London's commodity markets.

It would, however, be misleading to suggest that 'commodities' were the mainstay of business at these events. On the contrary, the majority of produce was processed or manufactured in some manner, but certainly commodities, known as 'avoirs de poids', implying sale by weight, such as grains, sugar, wool and various metals, were regular and intrinsic elements. Indeed, single commodity fairs were a common feature of the age. The most important of these specialised in wool, which was unchallenged as the most important commodity. Nonetheless, fairs for cloth, leather, livestock, cattle, horses, geese and sheep were organised and grew rapidly in stature. One of the most famous was the Weyhill Fair in Hampshire which specialised in sheep. It was a fair which grew tremendously over the years, such that its peak in the eighteenth century witnessed a turnover of around 140,000 sheep per day. The popularity continued for many years.

Only changing trade patterns, improving transport, and stricter health laws eroded the value of the fairs over time. Gradually, fairs were moved out of town centre locations and in time became more inclined towards entertainment than commerce. Only a few great fairs, such as that in Banbury, Oxfordshire, exist today. The majority have conceded to the tide of commercial change. Nonetheless, for the majority of the Middle Ages fairs were indispensable in terms of the dispersion and distribution of these commodities over regional and international levels. Together with the ubiquitous markets, they formed a solid and efficient marketing infrastructure and, in themselves, were responsible for significant advancements in many spheres. Banking, for example, was formalised in response to merchant demands and a relatively complex clearing system evolved during the Champagne Fairs described below.

The Champagne Fairs

The Champagne Fairs were organised in northern France and were undoubtedly the most prestigious fairs in Europe during the eleventh, twelfth and the beginning of the thirteenth centuries. As such, they were perhaps the best documented of all fairs at the time. They were quite revolutionary in practice, and had positive influences over many of their contemporaries. Thus the detour in this text is worth while. The Champagne region was centrally located with good access by river, thus endorsing its credentials as the hub around which much European trade revolved. Certainly the Fairs' importance was reflected insofar as much of the French road system of the age was organised to satisfy transport criteria. In time, the network grew to embrace Paris, the Low Lands, Italy, Germany and beyond.

Initially, the fairs, held in various towns in the region such as Provins and Troyes, were short in duration, although they lengthened in time to anything up to six weeks, each containing as many as fifty concurrent markets of specialised produce. As their durations became more prolonged they created an almost permanent summer fixture within the region, commencing on traditional saints' days and attracting participation from far and wide. They were first held in towns' streets, though the prosperity they proffered enabled the organisers to construct specialist stone-built market halls to protect traders and their wares from the elements.

Unquestionably, sophisticated organisation was elementary to a fair's success, and the Champagne Fairs proved over time to be superior in many respects. For instance, safe passage and conduct was assured by first the Count of Burgundy within his province, then by the King of France to include the entire country. The fairs were organised on a daily basis according to specific types of produce, and presented in an agenda type format. All contracts were in time recorded by notaries and guaranteed, in the event of default, by the Count himself. Such were their advantages that measures such as these were gradually gaining currency in many other fairs. Weights and measures became more standardised and where previous units were inappropriate they were replaced by more suitable modules such as the troy ounce (from the Troyes Fairs), used for quantifying precious metals.

One of the most innovative aspects of the organisation, however, was the evolution of relatively sophisticated clearing and credit systems. As each contract was formally recorded, principally to impose the pertinent tolls, every merchant was able to account for his purchases and sales and was more willing to grant credit against his debtors' inventories as rights of recourse and guarantees by the Count had been implemented. Gradually, transactions between merchants were effected less in cash and more in promise of payment upon the conclusion of the fair, at which time the merchants each collected debts and met their credit obligations. In time, this developed to the point where debts were carried forward to ensuing fairs and specific instruments of credit were introduced. Although this practice cannot be attributed directly to commodity trading, the commodity trade itself certainly gained great benefit from the less cumbrous methods of business conduct and the facility of credit. Without doubt they were major influences of general mercantile progress which consequently precipitated significant future growth and development.

The Middle Ages

The English Staple System

The English economy of the thirteenth century had expanded dramatically from that of the eleventh and twelfth centuries and by that time there had never been greater numbers of markets. However, there was a growing need for a more organised marketing system, particularly where exports were concerned. The response was the formation of a uniquely English institution - the 'Staple'.

Staple ports were introduced during the 1260's as appointed trade entrepots, though initially their use was not mandatory. The staple was a designated town, originally a port such as Bristol, London and Southampton, each with a customs office, but they were increased in number to fourteen to include inland towns such as York. They were exclusive trading centres for wool, grain, leather and metals (though admittedly the system was only really effective in the wool trade) which constituted depots and continuous markets. The coercion which evolved through various Ordinances was primarily economically motivated as it was easier to supervise export through prescribed channels, but it also facilitated easier customs collections, which was undeniably the principal motivation. The specialisation equated to concentration and the staples became regional capitals which, with regular supplies from their surrounding producers, placed their value beyond contention.

Of even greater significance were the political advantages inherent in their operation. Export licences were granted to specified individuals only, and could be instantly revoked at any time; and furthermore the staple system determined not purely domestic staple towns, but continental counterparts also. Therefore, the king of England was in a commanding position to dictate precise trade routes, volumes to maintain high prices, and types of raw materials to be exported. Politically, he was in possession of an unparalleled instrument with which to direct and subdue recalcitrant or opposing governments economically.

The system continued for around a century despite continuous pressure and opposition from those who considered it detrimental to free trade activity. Nevertheless, the duty system prevailed and remained operable even as late as the first half of the sixteenth century. More importantly, perhaps, its existence launched England into the primary league of mercantilist nations and provided wealth with which to explore and colonise in the coming centuries.

Towards Trader Specialisation

Significant change in the marketing system throughout England was inevitably accompanied by alterations in traditional merchanting and trading practices, and certainly the three hundred years to the close of the thirteenth century witnessed many such transformations. Itinerancy amongst traders was prevalent for much of the period, although the rise of towns, and demand for many commodities and raw materials, created the means for increasingly sedentary tendencies. This was, for many, of considerable advantage. Less time on the road equated to less risk from robbery, whereas residence invariably improved supply through continuity. The wiks were supplanted by the adoption of towns as largely permanent bases and the contact among merchants laid the foundations for cooperation and progress. The twelfth and thirteenth centuries recorded notable increases in the numbers of traders in response to demand through greater population, augmenting levels of wealth, and the rapid and widespread formation of markets and fairs.

Merchants were divided into one of two categories: international and domestic. The former, often of a wealthier disposition, frequented the great fairs throughout Europe in rotation, whilst the latter concerned themselves with more provincial trade, performing the vital task of distribution to the flourishing towns from their agricultural environs. Contact, certainly in the early part of this period, between the two classes was relatively infrequent as their functions were quite separate. However, the formation of guilds, described later in this chapter, resulted in ameliorated organisation of international trade and increased contact through association. Often merchants were further classified into 'best', 'middle class' and 'smaller' referring both to their importance and reputation. Pedlars and packmen were also widespread. They were small-scale opportunists who packaged their wares in black canvas packs and carried them upon their shoulders. In contrast to the more permanent local merchants, both pedlars and packmen were frowned upon as itinerants and beggars. They often sang to attract custom and roamed the countryside from market to market in pursuit of their trade.

Many of the more respectable merchants were frequently referred to as 'Cheapmen', which was subsequently corrupted to the surname 'Chapman'. It derives from the Anglo-Saxon word for market - cheap. Buying and selling was known as 'cheaping' from whence came this descriptive professional surname. It was also a word used to describe towns or areas within towns where markets were organised. Its derivatives, 'Chipping', which prefixes several English towns and Cheapside and Eastcheap in the City of London, remain as present-day reminders.

Expanding volume, particularly during the late twelfth and thirteenth centuries, was uniquely responsible for the trend among traders to specialise in a single commodity or group of related commodities. Specialisation invited a division of responsibilities where previously the entire process of provisioning markets and consumers was serviced by a single individual. Two examples of this are illustrated by transactions involving corn and wool. The movement of grain was, by the thirteenth century, subject to the involvement of the guildsmen who organised trade locally through various corn mongers. Where surpluses permitted they were able to provision the London markets and the larger ports for export. This was made possible by the advent of brokers, who arranged sales between merchants in return for a percentage of the transaction, in the form of commission.

Those concentrating on the wool trade similarly purchased from the producers in order to satisfy the Flemish and Italian merchants' demands by transporting the raw wool to the staple ports. Their success was largely due to their ability to respond to the demands of the market, and their ability to supply a variety of wools of various origins and qualities for specific customer requirements. Individual guilds were, conversely, restricted to the produce at their immediate disposal.

There were, however, certain drawbacks resulting from the rise of specialisation. First, markets were increasingly vulnerable to endeavours to corner supplies in order to augment prices. As each trade was conducted by fewer individuals with material interest, the potential to manipulate or control prices increased. The second problem was the natural inflation of prices from the extraction of profits at every stage of the trading chain by each of the 'middlemen' concerned. Solutions were never satisfactory to the entire community, as antagonistic interests were deep-rooted. Nonetheless, legislation was formulated to counter the problems of artificial price rises, but little could be imposed to dictate levels of profits under normal market conditions. The only attempt to counter this problem was the doctrine of 'just prices' which is described later in this chapter.

Specialisation was, however, as much enforced as it was preferred. Guilds, examined in greater detail below, assumed ever-increasing control over trade and became wholly responsible for trade within their towns; and were furthermore protected by charter. The staple system also saw the creation of the merchant staplers who, by licence, were granted the privilege of monopoly of all staple exports. Accordingly, they formed a public corporation, the Company of the Staple, governed by their own mayors and councils with the unqualified support of the Realm. Their powers were immense, with the ability to coerce sales at prices they dictated as an orthodox instrument of their enterprises. The Company of the Staple was a separate organisation from the Royal Staple which encouraged its formation. Therefore, although the merchant staplers were subordinate to the Realm, they were indispensable, but not irreplaceable.

Foreign merchants, meanwhile, were permitted to practise and remain in England for periods of up to forty days in the twelfth century, although this was later relaxed in their favour. During their sojourns they were theoretically obliged to reside with 'hosts', who witnessed their dealings. The practice was quite different, however. The Hosting Laws did not work and foreign merchants resided in England with little supervision. Additional restrictions prohibited their ability to sell on a retail level at markets (though this was permitted at fairs) and to purchase goods from other foreign merchants. This again was designed to protect domestic commercial interests and prevent uncontrolled exporting of the staples. It also conspired to yield further advantage to the myriad guilds of the day.

Merchant Guilds

Unlike the English staple system, guilds were medieval equivalents of ancient institutions and were prevalent throughout Europe. They were exclusively urban organisations which grew with the proliferation of towns and were granted commercial powers by licence from either the Crown or its lieutenants. The concept behind their constitution was both simple and highly discriminatory, for membership conferred corporate advantages and mutual liabilities. The principle was to create monopoly conditions; attract trade to each burg, and place guildsmen at an advantage over their outsider counterparts. The precise degree of guild privilege varied enormously from one to another.

Guilds were corporations of exclusive membership, although residence was not in many cases a prerequisite. Admission was subject to application and payment of an entrance fee which reciprocally incorporated rights to mutual insurance between the members and exemption from tolls within the town's markets. The most profound advantages resulted, however, from their routine operation.

The consistent objective of the guild merchants was the organisation of trade within their town, placing them in a commanding position to dictate trade practices and prices. Certain guilds, such as the Leicester Wool Guild, were at liberty to engage official brokers or woolmen to arrange sales outside their territory, and were allowed to sell on both retail and wholesale levels. Strangers, by contrast, were prohibited by law from selling on the open market, but were forced to sell their produce to the guildsmen, often at prescribed prices, though this again did not always work in the way it was intended. Non-guildsmen were, furthermore, prevented from purchasing raw wool and other staple commodities, and were additionally restricted as to the time and location at which they were permitted to practise.

Invariably, at ports, the guildsmen congregated to agree a fixed price upon the arrival of a cargo, and through the power of 'collective bargaining' the pre-determined price agreed amongst themselves was tendered for the produce, thus eliminating the element of negotiation and free market pricing. In some towns the staple commodities were subject to a monopoly constructed by syndicates of guildsmen who, upon disposal, shared profits equally between them. The monopolistic condition provided all members to 'right of lot' which enabled guildsmen to claim from a fellow guildsman provisions at the original cost price. The only criterion was that the claimant had to be present at the original sale. Perhaps the last organisational function was that of promotion of trade between their town and other towns, cities and ports, albeit they may have been placed at a disadvantage and, furthermore, that they were similarly restricted to selling on a strictly wholesale basis.

The subsidiary role of the guild merchant was the competent regulation of trade and the supervision of those who conducted it, although their subjectivity on the matter cast a somewhat dubious shadow over equitability. Internal disputes were not subject to outside legal jurisdiction, but were instead subject to arbitrational procedure. Altercations involving the general public were out of their control, however, and courts were organised to hear cases of this kind.

In a supervisory capacity the guilds were instrumental in dictating quantity and quality controls. Towns' reputations were paramount to their success and the imposition of acceptable standards was an important element; any adverse or corrupt transaction, outside the parameters of their privileges, was potentially most damaging, ultimately resulting in loss of custom or even boycott. The second branch to guild supervision was the imposition and collection of tolls, such as stallage on stalls, seldage on warehousing, pontage on bridges, and a fee for the use of the weigh beam (which was invariably the only scale to be legally accepted) each charged to outsiders in accordance with the terms of their charters. Progressively, however, tolls were systematically lifted on a reciprocal basis between guilds with particularly close affiliations and many tolls were vanishing from every-day practice altogether.

For individual guildsmen one major disadvantage was the doctrine of mutual liability, although this was gradually abolished during the thirteenth century. To the detriment of those on foreign territory, debts of members were liable to be imposed upon fellow members, even though they were never a party to the material transaction. In such events, their produce may have been sequestrated and sold in quittance of the outstanding debt. The obligation thus discharged restored accord, leaving the innocent guildsman to seek reparation from his defaulting colleague.

The Lex Mercatoria

The Law Merchant provided the transition from the unindited customary laws, with their origins in the tenth century, to formal and uniform codification. It evolved from the doctrines of litigation derived from the outcome of cases heard by the growing number of courts throughout England; and in so doing created the foundations for contemporary commercial jurisprudence. Generic application was not always one of its features, however, and early laws were wholly inconsistent with one another, each developing according to local cases, although in fairness, the axial principles relating to all trade activity were established. It was, rather, the complexity and frequency of disputes which exacted the appropriate reformation, commencing in the important commercial centres and the most prestigious of international fairs. Itinerant, yet experienced, judges studied laws and customs and gradually replaced their somewhat less knowledgeable counterparts. The consequence of specialisation, professionalism and wider jurisdiction was much improved systematisation and recording of events and cases, which, combined, created the framework for a unified and consistent legal regime. Special courts, such as those within the staple ports, presided over by the mayor, two constables and two additional alien assessors, were founded. Here disputes were rapidly settled according to universally acceptable European legal codes rather than specific or, in some cases, inapplicable customary laws.

The primary application of the Lex Mercatoria was at the fairs, at which speedy and equitable resolution of cases was essential. Forces of policemen accompanied every fair in order to maintain the peace and attempted to defuse superficial disputes which arose. However, some occasions warranted higher authority and rights to recourse which compelled investigation by the courts' officers, who were able to confiscate the chattels of the accused until a verdict had been reached. Fair courts were held throughout the day. Their judges were originally the towns' mayors, but in time the chief official was the bailiff. Each, however, presided over courts and decided cases with independent merchants as assessors. Later, however, cases were referred to the 'Courts of Piepowder' derived from the 'pieds poudres' or dusty feet of those concerned, at which itinerant judges evaluated the facts and dictated terms of resolution in an extremely practical and matter-of-fact manner. These cases, which led to the institution of International Law, provide a good illustration of the wider European influence and customs encouraged by the Normans and Plantagenets in particular.

The regulation of domestic markets was of equal importance, but their courts were far less glamorous and subject to somewhat questionable procedures of dispute reparation. Invariably the concession to hold a market was accompanied by the right, if not the obligation, to convene a court. When this was in the hands of those without material involvement, the incidence of justice prevailed. But not uncommonly it was the guildsmen who were accorded various privileges and thus they were frequently governors of the oligarchic towns' courts with subjective interests.

Equally problematical was the absence of records of cash transactions which exacerbated the difficulties of a just hearing and a successful verdict for outsiders. Nonetheless, 'tollbooths' at every market in the twelfth and thirteenth centuries accommodated officials collecting the numerous tolls and provided a forum for court tribunals. Markets also had stocks and ducking stools in the vicinity for offenders to receive public scorn and punishment. Some, such as the market at Bungay, added shackles to the market cross for public floggings. Evidently, justice was extremely rough and ready, with a tendency towards corruption. The alternative to the preferred sentence of corporal punishment was a fine levied as a measure of the crime, which was inherently more advantageous to the markets' organisers. Moreover, tolls tended more towards encumbrancy than equality if they were uncontested, and licences were withdrawn for unreasonable tolls and unfounded pecuniary punishments alike.

The Common Law Courts in England became demonstrably less effective and able to interpret the Law Merchant accurately or consistently. As a result, a separate legal department, the Court of Equity or Chancery, was established during the sixteenth century to provide an acceptable medium for civil actions and equitable reparations. It proved to be a valuable platform from which mercantile law was able to respond and develop.

The 'Just Price' Doctrine

Overtly, a conflict between buyers and sellers prevails in every commercial transaction as contradictory interests are at heart. However, though profit is an essential element of commerce, during the latter Middle Ages it was acceptable only insofar as consumers were not subjected to exorbitant or unnecessary increases in prices. Traders who extorted unreasonable profits were severely criticised for their deeds and though they were beyond punishment legally, if they operated within the law, they did receive considerable attention from philanthropic holy men and others who attempted to impose moral guidelines upon the ethics of trading. Saint Thomas Aquinas, the thirteenth century Dominican monk and theologian, endeavoured to be more precise in his definition of what was or was not morally acceptable. His doctrine was that of the 'just price' which sought to define the equilibrium between consumer protection and merchants' profit margins. On all accounts it was acceptable to trade at a 'reasonable' profit with freedom to practise at fairs or markets. However, apart from the essential function of provisioning communities, it was considered unethical to buy and sell purposely at various venues without regard for consumers' interests, if the sole intention was that of amassing profit. Naturally, the demarcation was very fine indeed, and one which was open to considerable interpretation. For whereas laws are universal, morals are personal standards which vary markedly between individuals. The doctrine of ' just prices' was, therefore, sound in principle, equitably set to benefit one and all, but its legal unenforceability made it extremely difficult to uphold.

Market Manipulation

Much of the Crown's attempts to banish manipulation and racketeering was through the 'market overt' principle. It insisted that all commodities for sale must be on open display and 'in a public and legally constituted market'. Thus private sales were outlawed and the practice of coercing participation at markets enacted under early Anglo-Saxon Law was reiterated. However, the terms of the market 'overt' principle went one step further as it addressed various contentions surrounding the transfer of title. One of the reasons for directing all sales through markets was the assumption that goods and commodities obtained through other means were likely to have been stolen. Those knowingly in possession of stolen goods were liable to the death penalty, so to protect buyers and their rights, the law protected only those buyers who were able to prove their purchases took place at market between sunrise and sunset. Buyers therefore acquired good title, provided they purchased provisions in good faith from their sellers. In simple terms this equated to transactions at markets. The principle of 'market overt' was unique to English Law, but it did not prevent other unsavoury activities from taking place. For example, those who intentionally attempted manipulation in some way, contrary to the principles of market overt and just price, fell into one of three categories: engrossers, forestallers and regraters, whose presence and operations were quite clearly delineated.

Engrossers purchased corn, and other commodities, in the field before harvest with the intention of storing them until supply was scarce and prices rose, when they would sell at a greater profit. From the thirteenth century economic practice and commercial ethics were closely related and the doctrine of 'just prices' prevailed wherever possible. It was, therefore, illegal to conceal produce secured in this way for indeterminate durations as it was contrary to public interest. Offenders were severely punished by fine or detention whilst their stocks were sequestrated and released onto the market.

Forestallers bought commodities on route to market at a price they considered lower than that likely to prevail upon their arrival. Their motivation was the realisation of short term profits. It was postulated that clandestine arrangements tended to prevent 'just prices' from being maintained, as forestallers instantaneously inflated the retail price of their acquisitions. Once again, confiscation and exile were imposed upon recalcitrants.

Regraters, by contrast, purchased at or immediately prior to the opening of a market at advantageous prices with the objective of subsequently re-selling to their profit. This practice was countered by rules which prevented purchase before dawn when markets traditionally commenced, which was the time many such bargains were struck.

Despite these outlawed activities and the concern they caused, the task of prevention was far from being adequately enforced. Invariably the guildsmen were at least in part responsible for such deeds, though fortunately for them, they exercised considerable influence within their towns, and were often well represented on the boroughs' councils. Whilst their powers were progressively diminishing, it was the rise of more uniform and objective domestic judicial proceedings which curtailed their ability to subvert justice, although manipulation of prices continued unabated for several centuries. The 'middlemen' active in pursuing these activities were loath to accept the criticism they attracted and pleaded that they possessed several redeeming qualities which are examined in greater detail in the following chapter.

Quantitative and Qualitative Standardisation

The creation of more unified trading conditions was complementary to, and essential for, the accommodation of wider involvement and increasing volumes. Standardisation was necessary not only for the equitable appraisal of quantity, but also the objective assessment of quality of saleable produce. Inspections of both were ritually performed for the assize under either guild supervision, which had vested commercial interests, or the municipal authorities under the charge of the town crier, who protected those of the consumer. Richard I, in 1197, attempted to standardise measures, in so doing replacing their infinitely variable counterparts which still persisted despite King Edgar's attempts during the tenth century to impose similar unification. Nonetheless, no nationwide standard existed. Each market had its own measures and traders were obliged to have their goods weighed and checked individually at each market they attended. (In fact, it was not until 1878 that many weights and measures were finally standardised. Only then was the length of one yard or the weight of one pound established. These official standards were then placed in London's Guildhall and have remained there ever since.) Sales were thus conducted according to true weight and each market incorporated its own public scales, invariably adjacent to the market cross, where tolls and taxes were also paid.

Perhaps the more important of the two measures of standardisation was the evaluation of certain commodities by grades according to purity or characteristic features. In the thirteenth century wool, for example, was first weighed then sealed to prevent tampering and was categorised into four basic grades reflecting its calibre. Metals, similarly, were also officially weighed, but were, furthermore, assayed to determine their fineness. The combination of quality calibration and quantity unification was responsible for two significant advances in market activity. On a retail level, it provided an equitable base which protected and encouraged consumer involvement; whereas on a wholesale level, merchants were able to rely upon the standards for transactions without having to resort to physical inspection of the commodity concerned. Any deficiency was protected by legal rights of recourse for false declarations or fraudulent assaying. Traders who broke the law were severely punished, often being placed in public stocks for lengthy periods, in addition to fines and confiscation of goods. The assurance of descriptive conformity assisted enormously in equitable market practices and operational efficiency. It was this very confidence which was so much in evidence during this period and a solid foundation from which to progress.

CHAPTER FOUR

The Renaissance and the Winds of Change

Following the ravages of plague and pestilence which indiscriminately killed millions of Britons and Europeans alike, the Renaissance is widely considered a period of significant beneficial change. It was characterised by intense commercial proliferation, perpetuating much of the mercantile confidence the latter part of the Middle Ages had instilled. This revival continued for several centuries until the seventeenth century, when profound alterations to Britain's political organisation were witnessed in response to burgeoning mercantile sophistication. Many market and trade developments were consolidated in their conceptual forms, but though consolidation was a feature of the Renaissance's four hundred year period, transformation was the unmistakable hallmark.

With the dawning of the fourteenth century came the transformation of many traditional economic policies. Perhaps the most noteworthy was the systematic transition over the ensuing centuries from regional or urban economies to one of a national regime. For this to take effect the inter-municipal guild affiliations had to be eroded in favour of wider national trade intercourse and economic unity. This undertaken, much of the discrimination and inequalities, which had for so long prevailed, were dismantled and in so doing the complexion of trade over the following centuries altered profoundly.

The Grain trade, for example, experienced a considerable metamorphosis, and its preponderance expanded with the centuries. Fourteenth century traffic was typically one of relatively localised proportions, though the perpetual growth of urban areas linked the towns to ever more remote satellites in order to satisfy their staple requirements. By the sixteenth century this trade had attained noteworthy international activity and grew in response to the demands of an increasing domestic population. It resulted not least from progressive agricultural specialisation which created a monocultural tendency in many areas. This was accompanied by supply fluctuations and developed into a situation whereby grain at certain times was less expensive to import than it was available domestically. Agriculture was changing, but there again, so too was the economic fabric of Britain.

Internal conflict was intensifying with the rise of industrialism. The agriculturalists competed directly with the entrepreneurial industrialists. The former sought protective measures to secure their livelihoods and perpetuate traditional culture; whereas the latter argued in favour of a relaxation of governmental intervention to develop a free market which would encourage lower prices as a result of an enhanced availability of raw materials

But it was not only the economy that was undergoing great change. For meanwhile the marketing system had to adapt to new economic factors to survive and flourish. The international fairs, for example, declined in importance first as exchanges for many commodities and subsequently for the trade in manufactured goods. This was due to the unprecedented demands of densely populated urban areas which necessitated greater and more regular provisions. They were gradually phased out as commercial affairs. Those which survived re-adopted their religious motives and became events of public entertainment and amusement.

The Renaissance was therefore a period of considerable development. Population was re-distributed in profile with towns growing at a great pace; agriculture was becoming specialised and monocultural; a more industrial outlook evolved: and the great trade fairs were in decline.

Each of these criteria directly affected the marketing of commodities; their fusion, however, highlighted the inadequacy of the marketing system which operated successfully in the Middle Ages, but under wholly different circumstances. As such, changes were inevitable.

Markets and their Practices

By the fourteenth century, markets, in response to changing agricultural patterns, were portraying increasingly specialist features in their operation. This trend encouraged a tremendous expansion in volume and with it came the origins of a rather more sophisticated internal organisation which, in turn, encouraged greater bonds between traders. Markets remained unconditional to commodity trade as the laws proffered to prevent forestalling (purchasing out of market) were continually reiterated, Despite their indispensability, however, they were modified in complexion and operation to provide for the changing economic conditions.

Stalls erected in streets on market days were gradually replaced by more permanent timber booths. At much the same time, many market crosses were embellished and some were completely covered to provide one or several rooms. Eventually, they developed into market halls. They were maintained by the market authorities, albeit some were initially donated by private individuals and displayed quite prominently the arms of the local landlord, or later that of the municipal corporation. Guildhalls, supported and surrounded by warehouses, were built to promote the specialised trade they patronised. The larger, more prosperous towns, meanwhile, supported both guild and market halls whereas stone-built exchanges were prominent features by the late sixteenth century. But their appearance was not the sole testimony to change. The number of markets, particularly those which dealt in grain and wool, declined quite dramatically between the fourteenth and sixteenth centuries. In Tudor and Stuart England, records indicate that only 750 or so were in existence; a marked decrease from the heyday of the Middle Ages. This contraction may be attributed to a notable fall in population sequent to the rapacious plague, agricultural specialisation and also in part to improving transport facilities, but it does not imply a similar trend in trade activity. The profile of such trade may have altered but its volume was continually on the increase.

The re-definition of trade in commodities can also be attributed to the growth of towns which, following the conclusion of the plague, continued to rise in importance and embrace, unremittingly commanding trade over wider distances. Later still, during the 18th and 19th centuries, the number of markets diminished again due to the system of turnpikes and then the arrival of railways. Consequently, the smaller village markets were culled from the ranks, while others survived, but became outlets for secondary agricultural produce. In their place were bakers and other tradesmen who frequented the towns' markets and serviced the smaller communities. Significantly fewer markets therefore existed in the latter part of the period; corn sales were exclusive to designated market towns and the practice of buying or leasing a stand in market halls became a common feature.

The trade in corn, as we have seen, was first directed to markets and later towards corn exchanges. However, although most sales were effected by immediate bulk transfer, the practice of selling by sample was becoming increasingly commonplace. It was considerably more economical, as transport, by either carter or farm hand, was avoided, which thus made the journey to market inherently easier. It attracted much criticism, however, as transactions were completed away from the market, albeit they had been negotiated and concerted there. But there was always a distinct possibility that substantially more changed hands than had been recorded. Clandestine transactions were a convenient method of evading taxation, and the buyers for their part were able to bargain for more advantageous prices. Reciprocally beneficial arrangements such as these were difficult to prevent and continued for some time unabated.

Nonetheless, markets were still strictly supervised, following customary guidelines. During the sixteenth century the Justices of the Peace convened meetings among the grain sellers on the day prior to the market. Their task was collectively to determine the maximum price at which grain could be sold, based upon their assessment of deliverable supply. On market day all vendors, whether or not they were present at the meeting, were compelled to comply with these price directives. This action testifies to a noteworthy alteration in pricing policy. For whereas the 'just price' doctrine was directed more towards moral guidelines, the prices fixed by the Justices of the Peace were legally enforceable. The system was designed to relieve the poor of the burden of inflation, as they were subjected to a public prescription of wages as far back as 1351.

Markets were, therefore, designed to be extremely equitable affairs, organised to provide every opportunity for the consumers to purchase their requirements in advance of the merchants. The sales, which commenced at nine a.m., were first open to householders, who were permitted to purchase up to a maximum of two bushels of corn. At eleven o'clock the phalanx of merchants was admitted and 'free trade' was instigated. Any business concluded during the day was subject to transport on the day; any other movement could have been construed as being contrary to the laws governing forestalling and, if this was proven, the produce was seized and the offender interned.

Ostensibly, the marketing of grain was streamlined quite considerably over the period. By the close of the seventeenth century, stonebuilt corn exchanges were endemic as primary markets and have altered very little since. The trade in wool witnessed similar transformations in its operation, though the rise in the status of cotton in the eighteenth century heralded an end to its pre-eminence. Markets in this specialist form were important cogs in Britain's economic machinery, but the tides were turning towards a freedom in commodity marketing and the following centuries were testimony to this fact.

Trading Techniques

The sophistication of markets during the Renaissance demanded a corresponding increase in complexity of the trading techniques employed.

The Renaissance and the Winds of Change

Despite opposition, the practice of selling by sample remained a feature of market activity, but the constant danger was one of non-execution by either party compounded by the inconvenience and risk of returning to market. In response to these conditions, merchants of the Renaissance introduced the 'Denarius Dei' or God's penny, as deposits for transactions of this nature in order to bind the parties to the terms agreed. The principle was derived from the use of the 'festuca', which was a token employed to represent the ownership of land. Contracts settled by this method were 'uberimae fidei' - in the utmost good faith and subsequent withdrawal was subject to the forfeiture of the deposit and a fine, in the case of the purchaser defaulting, whereas sellers were required to pay double the customary amercement.

The fourteenth century also records mounting exercise of forward trading techniques which were introduced during the latter part of the thirteenth century. There were essentially two types of arrangement with major differences in their execution. The first practice was similar in many respects to the Roman system of deferred delivery, although their contemporary exponents did not sell the crop to a bona fide purchaser in advance of delivery, but instead mortgaged their crops to a financier to discharge taxation or service obligations. Though in this respect their motivations coincided, the difference was simply that the latter-day arrangement did not prematurely sell the produce, as this would have been in breach of the laws governing forestalling, but the merchandise was itself used as collateral for the loan. Upon harvest the farmer still held title to his crops, but having sold them at market, he was liable to repay his debt.

More akin to the principles of modern-day forward trading, however, were the advance contracts prevalent in the wool trade. Occasionally, the larger, more influential landlords sold their wool forward, based upon their anticipated clips. Wool was not subject to the same restrictions as grains and other staple commodities as it was, by this time, no longer an open market commodity, and traders were at liberty to satisfy their inventory requirements in a relatively unmolested manner. The contract, invariably settled by the use of the Denarius Dei, was frequently valid for several years at a pre-determined price and pre-arranged delivery location. It did not, however, embody terms of quantification, as it was difficult to predict with any degree of accuracy the size of the clip. However, this practice was coming to a steady conclusion as the terms of the English Staple were being dissolved. Nonetheless, it was perpetuated for a time by the woolmen, but resulted all too often in disastrous consequences. Their error was simply the inconsistency between their forward sales and their forward purchases, which exposed them to a considerable risk from fluctuating prices when their obligations did not correspond. As these advance contracts became regarded by many as counter-productive the woolmen relied increasingly on their monopoly to secure prices and less on the somewhat risky method of forward contracting with which they had flirted.

The Dissolution of Guilds and the Rise of Licensing

The institution of the guild merchant during the Middle Ages was gradually exhausting its utility, particularly where commodities were concerned, and if the transition from a municipal to a national economy were to be secured, it had to be accomplished with the sacrifice of the discriminatory barriers which had been erected. Guilds were alleged to be contrary to free trade and their custom of placing outsiders at a disadvantage was patently restrictive. However, the problem was intensified by the preclusion of purchasing ex-market, i.e. forestalling, which served only to emphasise the monopoly they possessed over local trade.

The London merchants were highly critical of this situation and attempted to relieve themselves from the asphyxiating grasp of the provincial guilds. Their objective was simply to enjoy some exemption from guild restrictions and create for themselves a national market liberated from protectionist guild enterprises.

London merchants had a powerful tool at their disposal - the size of the metropolis' population. It was its exigencies which quite naturally inflated the price of the paliable grains and other commodities. As such, considerable leverage was available to the capital's merchants whose needs were high and who were able to pay above the odds. Despite their ability and willingness, if need be, to pay a premium to the producers for their grain provisions, it was not until the sixteenth century that their exemption from tolls and other restrictive practices, supported by legislation, eroded the guild monopolies and the road of progress had been successfully paved.

The eradication of guilds was but a single constituent part of the transformation which was set to take place, and the regiments of middlemen were the recipients of similar reform. It was commonly held that middlemen possessed few redeeming qualities and their existence served only to manipulate prices to the detriment of the consumers. Laws were already evolving during the fourteenth century to prevent indiscriminate buying of wool for re-sale. Private individuals were largely inhibited from purchasing raw wool, but this only served to highlight the advantages of the merchant staplers and the cloth manufacturers. The re-iteration of this law over the following centuries had already set precedents to curtail the activities of the unpopular middlemen.

Similar restrictions on the grain trade were promulgated in a statute of 1552 However, the value of the middlemen was slowly realised and the laws were designed not so much to prohibit their involvement, as to restrain them from inordinancy.

In 1549, guilds were being increasingly dissolved upon Edward VI's instructions. In their place he established municipal corporations by royal charter. They were bestowed with manorial rights, including that to hold a market, and invariably emerged from the medieval guilds which they replaced. While some corporations and some of the more powerful guilds existed concurrently, much of the power was transferred, together with guild property, to the newly created corporations. They became (and have remained ever since) the sole authority over markets and were ideally placed to regulate and maintain the machinery of trade.

In part, this resulted in the initiation of a licensing system administered by municipal authorities. Licences were obtainable upon subscription for terms of one year, though applicants frequently had to be male, over thirty years of age, married, and a resident or at least three years' standing of the town where they applied. Clearly, the authorities were selective in their approach towards the granting of licences - as indeed was necessary. Licences were all important. Indeed, these documents were essential as they allowed access to markets and the ability to transact business. In view of the stringent laws countering forestalling and the like which prevented general participation, licences conferred tremendous advantage on those who possessed them. In so doing, they gradually, if reluctantly, legitimised their activities to the satisfaction of all concerned.

Middlemen

Public opinion had always tended to condemn middlemen such as the wool staplers and corn merchants. They were despised for their allegedly avaricious activities which, as we have witnessed, were thought to be directed to the manipulation of prices and the control of supplies. Even at the end of the Renaissance they were viewed with suspicion as engrossers, regraters and forestallers by the greater proportion of the populace. Such was the fervent opposition to their enterprises that Queen Elizabeth I wrote a letter to the Archbishop of Canterbury requesting him to include a passage in his sermons to condemn those who practised in these capacities. Measures such as these were extremely popular with the general public, needless to say, though the middlemen denied these allegations, stating in defence that they were too few in number and the market was far too large for them to create artificial conditions, much less sustain them. They claimed, furthermore, that their actions were in favour of public interest rather than antagonistic to it, and their self-appraisal was gaining credence with numerous economics scholars.

Their role was highly contentious, but despite widespread disapproval they were indispensable to the stability of national markets, based upon the theoretical performance of five separate functions.

i) Manufacturing centres and urban areas were not always favourably located vis-a-vis agricultural or mining regions which presented problems of consistent, adequate supplies of many of the staples. Though the guilds were active in meeting these needs as best they could, they were often restricted by their affiliations with others. Therefore insufficient supplies, or those of a sub-standard nature, were potentially disastrous to their towns' prosperity and well-being. The middlemen, by contrast, were, if permitted, at liberty to purchase wherever they chose, and in so doing they improved links between producers and consumers.

ii) Wool staplers were in a position to cater for specialist requirements, the performance of which minimised wastage, and thereby expense. As a fleece commonly comprises wool of as many as ten different grades, to the clothiers engaged in specialist production, whether it were fine cloth for the wealthy or coarser cloth for the general public, purchasing entire fleeces was grossly inappropriate relative to their raw material requirements. By purchasing complete fleeces they obtained wool unsuitable for their trades which they had to pay for, and dispose of. In effect, the waste directly and unnecessarily contributed to the inflation of costs. The wool staplers, conversely, were in a position to sort the wools according to their grades, and supply them to qualitative as well as quantitative criteria. In this way, they prevented unnecessary wastage and therefore minimised the direct cost of raw materials.

iii) Forestallers were always bitterly opposed, though even they had redeeming qualities. Transport and journeys to and from markets remained a lengthy and comparatively expensive exercise for producers to undertake and one which was unavoidably reflected in the market price. The forestallers, by frequenting the production location and purchasing there, ostensibly avoided the clearly unnecessary expense of moving produce unreasonably, thus reducing the wholesale price. All things considered, they saved considerable time and expenditure, and in so doing invariably secured the most advantageous prices.

iv) Similarly, engrossers and regraters tended to stabilise wider markets by acquiring and releasing merchandise as prevailing conditions dictated. They bought produce where supply was plentiful and prices were moderate and sold on subsequent occasions where demand exceeded supply and prices were correspondingly higher. To this end, they regulated supply irregularities, allowing prices to be adjusted to more equitable levels.

v) Wool staplers additionally granted beneficial payment terms, extending long credit to the clothiers, whereas the producers frequently sought immediate and full settlement, though this was not exclusively the case. Indeed, some wool growers offered extremely attractive payment conditions. Nonetheless, in general terms, the middlemen, with their somewhat more commercial attitudes, permitted cloth producers to manufacture their merchandise and sell it at market, at which time they discharged their outstanding debts. Simultaneously, replacement supplies were obtained and further credit bestowed. In this way, the rolling credit offered by the wool staplers relieved many of the fiscal difficulties the clothiers encountered, thereby fostering goodwill and encouraging production. Without this facility, it is postulated that many clothiers would have perished under the financial strains, ultimately inhibiting economic growth through large scale unemployment and diminished commercial activity.

In spite of the advantages middlemen were in a position to provide, they were continually viewed with suspicion, and if alternatives could be promulgated, they were always preferentially implemented. For instance, corn hoarding, reputedly the practice of the engrossers, was bitterly condemned by governments, and those found in breach upon investigation were compelled to sell at market under price supervision. It was, however, a none too easy task to administer, as magistrates were frequently producers who escaped the letter of the law.

Despite certain short-comings, fourteenth century municipal authorities established town granaries from bequests of money and grants from local governments to counter manipulation and regulate prices. Later, in the fifteenth century, the Crown attempted to implement the system nationally by purchasing grain when its price fell, storing it throughout the country, and releasing it when scarcity demanded. The concept, good though it was, fell short of the mark and attracted considerable criticism on two counts. First, the cost of the operation to the extent of efficacy was exorbitantly high and deployed treasury reserves which could otherwise be spent. Second, producers regarded it as a mechanism of suppressing prices to artificially low levels which effectively discouraged production. As a result, supplies contracted and prices inevitably rose to the extent that they were consistently above those prevailing prior to the introduction of the system.

The resistance to middlemen slowly disintegrated in face of the complexity of economic problems and the continual growth of towns during the sixteenth century. The wool trade had all restrictions over middlemen removed in a law of 1624. In so doing, it laid the foundations for the legitimate involvement of regraters and engrossers as they actively aided supply and, therefore, price difficulties. It was then possible either to buy and re-sell at markets, or store produce providing it had been obtained at market and thereafter re-sold upon the proviso that it did not re-appear on the same market for three months' duration.

In reality it was the tempering of opposition which permitted middlemen to practise lawfully at markets, but little relaxation was afforded to forestallers. It was not until 1597 when carte blanche exemption was granted by the Privy Council to the London merchants that they were able to forestall markets. London merchants were in an unassailable position in the English domestic economy, a command which ignited substantial conflict with their provincial counterparts. They were able to purchase both ex- and at market, at a time when the provincial middlemen were still prevented from either engrossing or regrating. Of all the restrictions, those governing forestalling were the most difficult to repeal. It was not until the eighteenth century, through the rise of laissez-faire economic theory, that all such prohibitions were revoked, as they were widely accepted to be inhibitive and discouraging of trade, and therefore, supply.

Cartels and Rings

Producers of many commodities were awakening to the notion of manipulating supplies and prices for significant commercial gain, to the detriment of their obligations to their nation's economy, and the institution of the 'just price' doctrine. By the end of the sixteenth century, they were active in co-operating with one another to create artificial market conditions and control trade activity, but in so doing they stirred much governmental investigation. Irrespective of the suspicion they aroused, their associations were built on firm foundations of mutual profits, and some continued for several centuries.

Ostensibly, producers affiliated their interests in exclusive syndicates whereby collectively they agreed production quotas and therefore established artificial prices. In the copper and tin mining industries it was comparatively easy to orchestrate matters as the few companies engaged in these activities at the time made general agreements perfectly viable. The trades in wool, grain, iron and coal were substantially more difficult to control, requiring far more sophisticated organisation. Collectively and independently, traders and producers conspired to gather information on supplies and prevailing prices in order to manipulate markets to their financial advantage. This was effected by eliminating or suppressing competition through the bulk release of merchandise at attractively low prices to prevent foreign imports and sustained purchasing of surplus provisions to corner markets. Though their motives illustrate a rather dubious alteration in commercial outlook, they are indicative of the radical transformations of the era and presage a variety of other developments in the future.

Ancillary Professions

As a consequence of ever-increasing sophistication of trade through volume-induced specialisation, came the foundation and genesis of numerous peripheral professions whose enterprises contributed much to the huge progress achieved during the Renaissance. Merchants were becoming, increasingly sedentary in their activities, not purely for the reasons previously stated, but due to the tendency to conduct business at particular markets on a more regular basis with associates who were mutually familiar with one another. This continuity minimised the need for frequent journeys to markets where the deals were struck, in favour of the engagement of others with well defined responsibilities.

Carters, as we have observed, were commonplace by the end of the thirteenth century and were employed extensively to collect and deliver merchandise as appropriate. Couriers, meanwhile, were introduced during the fourteenth century, initially with the task of forewarning local communities of the arrival of their merchant employers, but also, to an extent, to make purchases at some markets in advance of their arrival. This was facilitated by the more uniform standardisation of quality, measured by grades or fineness, which signalled the ability of merchants to purchase sight unseen if the price was attractive, in the full, confident knowledge that the produce was legally bound to correspond to its specification. Couriers, therefore, carried out many of the routine functions merchants were obliged to perform, but they also provided an additional, invaluable service. Much of the merchants' professionalism was an expertise in when to buy and sell, in a manner which did not breach any laws, to their best advantage. Previously they relied upon their instincts, experience and word of fellow merchants to determine when and where they bought and sold, though evidently this was a somewhat risky exercise. The wealthier merchants were becoming considerably more professional in their approach and instituted an intelligence system through their couriers. Each was based in a prescribed area or town, and from their observations of market supplies and prices they reported frequently to their employers, who determined what action, if any, need be taken. Evidently, the use of efficient communications, in whatever form, was an essential factor in market sophistication, and illustrates the stabilisation it both encouraged and permitted.

Couriers were retained for relaying information between markets, but the act of buying and selling was rapidly becoming the domain of specialist agents or factors, whose livelihoods were derived from the performance of these duties for several clients. They were particularly prominent in London and other European cities, where markets were insatiable in their requirements and provided merchants with a profitable excursion from local transactions. These factors often bought permanent stands at markets, such as London's premier grain market at Bear Quay, to ensure accessibility. Some were exclusive to associations of traders and factors, which although permitted the universal right to trade there, prohibited direct outside personal involvement. The agents therefore executed business among themselves for their principals in return for a commission of around two to three per cent of the transaction's value. Their revenues were derived exclusively from the transaction of business for others, but their privileged position no doubt encouraged some to adopt a rather more speculatory stance in order to increase their income.

For most merchants the ideology of risk avoidance was gaining considerable currency, as many had perished from the existence of risk which continually threatened the very foundations of commerce. The protection of mercantile interests was addressed in part by the arrival of insurance at the beginning of the century to protect loans and merchandise in transit. Transport insurance was initially only available for maritime traffic, though this was extended in time to embrace overland trade routes also. Premiums were levied according to the type and speed of the mode of transport, the size, nature and value of the cargo, distance and destination amongst other factors. But this insurance was by no means inexpensive. It accounted for as much as twenty per cent of the value of the merchandise, even over relatively minor distances. Effectively, however, the premium was absorbed into, and reflected in, the ultimate market price which inevitably created a degree of inflation. Notwithstanding this, the facility of reimbursement in the event of loss was popularly attractive, and was gradually adopted by all engaged in sea transport. The compensation for the rise in price was regularity of supplies.

Methods of Price Stabilisation

The responsibility of price stabilisation continued as a part of governmental direction. In an age when more sophisticated enterprise fostered the use of numerous agents and outside professions, each of which put pressure on an upward movement of prices, the Crown and its government were obliged to remedy their effects in order to regulate the economy. The imposition of tariffs was fraught with damaging consequences as they tended to inhibit production rather than stimulate it. Therefore, successive governments saw the control of supply as a prerequisite to economic prosperity. By encouraging production, prices could be maintained at lower market rates, whilst the increased volume of disposable commodities compensated for lower market prices. To an extent, however, middlemen contributed towards the regularisation of provisions, though in times of scarcity they were incapable of enacting radical solutions.

The Corn Act of 1670 re-inforced this approach. Quite simply, it permitted exports in periods of abundance, and placed a variable duty on imports. The rates were high when domestic production was adequate in order to inhibit imports, and low when a shortfall existed, so as to supplement domestic supplies. It was not, however, the ideal solution. As prices were relatively low in times of surplus, producers invariably abstained from corn production in favour of other agricultural produce. Consequently, production tended to vary over a three or four year cycle and prices oscillated in tandem. As this had de-stabilising effects, a remedy had to be found. Either farmers had to regulate their production to meet domestic demand in order to maintain prices, or the government had to devise a method of guaranteeing prices. As exports were the key to augmenting national wealth, the government was duty bound to support prices financially in order to maintain supply, stabilise domestic prices and secure exports.

In 1673, bounties, designed to regulate domestic supply and price, were introduced on corn to encourage domestic production. They contrasted with subsidies, as the latter were granted on all exports over and above the price secured in the open market. The rate at which the bounties applied was directed by the government, which monitored market rates. When they fell to a proscribed level, implying surplus supply over demand, the bounties were introduced and a subsidy was paid on all exports. When harvests were inadequate on the home market, imports were invited through the relaxation of duties which reduced the domestic market price. In any event, the government was in a much enhanced position to control supply; this rather than eliminating price fluctuations, served to arrest them to a substantial degree.

Bounties also assisted speculative activity, though admittedly not extensively. Exporters collected bounties in accordance with the prevailing conditions, but rather than supplying markets abroad, cargoes were stored for varying durations and re-imported in times of domestic scarcity. In this way, they returned extraordinary profits as they purchased when prices were low in England, reaped the benefit of the subsidy and subsequently repatriated stocks when home market prices had risen significantly. In spite of transport costs they proved to be extremely profitable ventures.

Irrespective of this, bounties endured critical opposition, none more vehement than from Adam Smith, who challenged the trade protectionist policies they embodied. Nevertheless, they continued long into the eighteenth century, but mounting criticism of embargoes and the rise of free marketing were elementary to their eventual revocation.

Inns and Coffee Houses

It is widely acknowledged that the coffee houses of the seventeenth century were responsible for the formation of numerous trade associations which developed into many of the City of London's financial institutions. Though it seems somewhat incongruous that such important institutions could emanate from such humble beginnings, the use of coffee houses as markets was by no means an invention of the period. The fifteenth and sixteenth centuries equally had markets held in the congenial surroundings of many inns, and despite widespread disapproval they accounted for a quite noteworthy private trade. Undoubtedly repealing the forestalling laws against London merchants provides one reason for their preponderance. Informal though the environment was, it certainly did not reflect the conduct of trade carried on there. For not only did the innkeepers provide accommodation, but stores for merchandise were often provided, as were private rooms where business was transacted. Invariably, innkeepers acted as brokers for their patrons in their absence in return for a small consideration, and some were privy to all contracts and not infrequently underwrote them in some way. Their involvement in this capacity was a natural extension of the laws compelling foreigners to have witnesses to their dealings in the Middle Ages.

In many ways, the coffee houses were successors of these popular resting places and assumed many of their traditional roles. The transition, certainly in London, was not a fluid affair, but one which temporarily resided in the cavernous hall of Sir Thomas Gresham's Royal Exchange, which was accorded Royal assent by Elizabeth I on 23rd January 1571. Its architectural style and concept of operation were similar to the then recently inaugurated Bourse in Antwerp. Incorporated within its walls were walkways which separated various trading disciplines, where news and information was exchanged and business conducted at frequent, prescribed times. Merchants both inside the Royal Exchange and in its vicinity tended to congregate in specific areas for specific trades, often because their separation was a legal requirement. But the major and, to all intents and purposes, insoluble drawback of the Royal Exchange came ironically from its very popularity, and increasing numbers of merchants made trading simply impossible. Symptomatic of this intolerable situation was the gradual abandonment of the Royal Exchange as the primary market.

Instead traders, escaping the overcrowded conditions, resorted to meetings at specified locations which became markets within a market. Off London's Cheapside are streets which bear testimony to this fact, with Bread Street, Poultry, Milk Street and Ironmonger Lane in existence to this day. But other merchants tended to meet in the various 'coffy huisen' or coffee houses which were much in acclaim in Amsterdam where they originated.

In London, the first coffee house was opened in 1652 in Cornhill, but they expanded in number at a tremendous pace, each one attracting a peculiar clientele or merchant specialist in a particular business. They were private members' clubs which, upon payment of an annual subscription, permitted comprehensive use of all the facilities to hand. Owners provided newspapers, shipping lists, information from ports, news of prices attained elsewhere, boards for records and benches for their congregation and some, such as the Jerusalem Coffee House in Cowper Court, the meeting place most favoured by metal merchants, even incorporated a sawdust ring for those wishing to trade. They were in every respect ideal for the service they provided, though once again sheer weight of numbers dictated that movement to new premises was overdue. The members subsequently formed associations among themselves, capitalised companies to provide and promote marketplaces, and the transition to the plethora of city institutions we recognise today was founded.

CHAPTER FIVE

The Rise of Free Market Economics

The arrival of the eighteenth century was accompanied by continuing and significant changes in the economic and political framework of the most powerful dominion in the world - Britain. It was one of unprecedented change, witnessing the final stage of the transition from the traditional agriculturally orientated economy through to the Industrial Revolution and the conversion to greater manufacturing dependence. Ever-mounting opposition to governmental control of trade divided old principles from contemporary theories: increasing pressure was brought to bear upon the government to temper its involvement and orchestrate a less discriminatory approach whereby inordinate restriction was withdrawn and free movement of raw materials and commodities was permitted. Population, meanwhile, expanded unceasingly as ever. Domestic corn production slumped below demand and England was compelled to import consistently for the first time in over a century.

The effects were evident in every facet of routine life and naturally with these reformations came radical alterations in the marketing of commodities. The modifications in commodity trading were natural responses to developments in economic activity: changes which culminated in fundamentally new approaches, Acknowledging that many features of these novel Marketing methods were progressions from medieval or ancient origins, they were nonetheless revolutionary in their collective form. The development concluded with the establishment of two entirely different forms of commodity trading which we still recognise today and are described in detail below. They were fashioned from the emergent political regime and the very nature of their trades, responding principally to three important elements.

First, the abandonment of the self-sufficiency policy, due to the proliferation of population, saw the lifting of many laws which prevented the free traffic of many staple commodities and the revocation of various subsidies and duties. The tenor was undeniably one directed towards a 'laissez-faire' economy which transferred the responsibilities of production and distribution to the industrial and agricultural communities. However, with the removal of governmental control came the collapse of relative price stability as the management of trade balances, previously secured through supportive subsidy and preventive duty, expired. The consequence was a period of volatile price movements reacting to market forces which meant the traders and merchants of commodities were exposed to considerable commercial risks.

Secondly, the spoils of colonisation and global exploration were permeating through to the home market in ever increasing volumes. New commodities abounded in popularity and general markets were rapidly diminishing in their ability to cope with the unprecedented volume and variety. Sugar, which had originally been an eastern product, was imported from the Americas and the West Indies. It enjoyed a remarkable growth in demand which witnessed an annual trade in 1800 amounting to some 150,000 tons - a fifteen-fold increase within a century! Tea was imported from China and India as early as 1610, but the English had developed a unique western partiality for it and the volume of its trade increased enormously; coffee arrived in London during the seventeenth century following its appearance in Vienna and Paris, gave its name to the popular meeting places in Amsterdam and then London, and although initially a Muslim commodity, it became of major agricultural importance to the West Indies; cocoa was principally a South American discovery which rose in popularity in French and Spanish courts in the form of chocolate, later becoming manifest in the United Kingdom. Collectively, these new commodities were instrumental in the creation of new markets characteristic of trade patterns, and avoided much of the evolution which the grain and metal trades had experienced over several centuries.

The third component was the increasing distance over which trade was conducted. Even at the height of the Roman Empire the extent of trade, particularly sea-borne, did not compare with the geography of Britain's commercial operations over this period. But trade over such distances was not without its drawbacks. The ramifications of uncertain or infrequent supply were potentially disastrous, and further exacerbated some of the difficulties the merchants faced. Coinciding as it did with the government's decision to give up much of its control of trade, the risks encountered by merchants were augmented to levels never seen before. New trading methods were therefore pre-requisite.

At much the same time as these new and quite radical commodity marketing methods were being introduced, the gradual transference of powers over markets away from the Crown and the lords of the manors towards the Local Authorities was taking place. This transition occurred over a number Of years, but was made obligatory upon the passing of the Public Health Act in 1875, which ensured the ownership and management of markets was almost exclusively in the hands of the Local Authorities. Apart from a few private markets operating, even then, under Local Authority licence, all markets became thenceforth the responsibility of Local Authorities throughout Britain and this continues to the present day.

The Re-Establishment of Forward Trading

The degree of paliable grain price variation, due to supply oscillations and political manoeuvres, resulted inevitably in a risk which not only threatened the financial stability of the merchants who dealt in these staple commodities, but it had potentially serious repercussions on the economy, which was faced with the continual barrage of the population explosion and consumer demand. There was a profound need for measures to control fluctuations in prices in order to reduce risks; ensure consistent provisions; and thus regulate the country's economic foundations. In the event, it was the application of the forward contract which fulfilled many of these requirements and thus signalled a major stride forward in commodity market development. Despite an entirely radical change in trading practices, many of its features can be traced back centuries into the past, and although part of this chapter will focus on the methods and operation of this trading phenomenon, every attempt will be made to illustrate its origins and parallels in bygone times.

The practice of selling agricultural crops in advance of harvest had, as we have seen, been a preoccupation of farmers for some fifteen hundred years, first by Roman, then medieval landowners who were forced to mortgage their production in order to meet their taxation liabilities. There had also been instances when sales were contracted forward through periodic arrangements of price to ensure profitability, although this was rarely, if ever, quantified in respect of deliverable supplies. However, the character of eighteenth century forward trading was concerned neither with premature realisation of capital nor the forward re-sale of commodities on a retail level. Moreover, it was designed to satisfy two essential criteria; first, to mitigate, as far as possible, the risks inherent in periods of volatile price movements on a strictly wholesale basis; and second, simultaneously to ensure continuous supplies. Conceptually, therefore, it was fundamentally different.

The Benefits of Forward Trading and Exchanges

Evidently, traders and merchants would have been reluctant to engage in forward trading unless there were compensatory circumstances. The motivation was the assurance of supplies at pre-determined times in the future and at agreed prices, which were quite revolutionary concepts. But once understood and applied, they were invaluable to buyers and sellers alike, and rapidly became a ritual part of trading activities. However, to arrive at a better understanding of the advantages of forward trading, it is probably best to examine the basic mode of operation.

At much the same time as forward trading was established, corn was of unrivalled agricultural importance but demand continued to outpace production. Accordingly, imports, permitted through the dismantling of economic barriers, were not only intrinsic to the trade but they were, furthermore, augmenting in volume. English farmers witnessed fluctuations in price of unparalleled frequency and extent. The constant threat of climatic changes and seasonal variations created periods of relative abundance and scarcity on markets. This was potentially highly damaging, as the price the farmers may have been able to secure could have been only of marginal profitability, or worse still, less than the collective costs of production. The millers, though benefiting in such circumstances, were by contrast in similar difficulty when the supply was deficient and were equally ill-positioned to absorb the inflated cost of their raw materials. The solution was the forward contract. It was fixed as to the quantity, price and delivery date and thereafter concluded upon the physical transfer or the consignment. In this way, the farmer no longer had to concern himself with constant price and supply variations. He was thus in a position to negotiate in advance a price which ensured an acceptable measure of profit.

Equally, the miller or merchant was able to dispense with the difficulties of erratic price patterns which had previously plagued him, whilst securing future supply in the process. In so doing, the seller forfeited the potential of extraordinary profits when supply was short and prices high, while buyers conceded similar advantages when market conditions were reversed. Accordingly, each party avoided many of the inherent risks and in so doing, secured both supply and price. Abstention from this practice, whether by buyer or seller, was highly risky and the transaction reverted to a state of pure speculation.

So much for the value of forward trading, but what of the reasons for the organisation of exchanges? Forward trading is a natural extension of markets convened for on-the-spot cash transactions. Therefore concurrent markets existed between 'spot' delivery and Forward contracts. Corn Exchanges became an increasingly common sight in many market towns, Most were built between 1840 and 1870, usually by private companies under licence from the local authorities. They were often built on the main market places themselves and were of classical appearance, normally surmounted by the ancient figure of Ceres.

They engaged in both dimensions of trading but their indispensability was thus not dependent upon either discipline. Rather, they were more simply responsible for establishing and maintaining contact between buyers and sellers, farmers and factors. Through the concentration of participants which they brought about, the efficacy and simplicity of conducting business were amplified to their mutual advantage. If volume of transactions is the acid test of the satisfaction of all criteria, the acceleration and amplitude of transactions accorded at these exchanges is testimony to the favour they found. Almost immediately, forward contracting proved to be an intrinsic and popular trading method with their patrons.

Others were organised by way of a trade association which governed both membership and regulation. Many such affiliations were established between traders whose mutual interests led them to the formation of various commodity exchanges for routine trading matters. They were 'closed' membership affairs which exacted an annual subscription and a levy on all transactions for the maintenance and promotion of the exchange itself. Their internal regulation was conducted under the auspices of elected officials to committees, which entailed among a number of other duties ensuring observation by their members of codes of conduct, setting accounting, disciplinary and arbitration procedures, and the election of new members. What is important to note is their autonomy over self-regulation upon the condition that statute laws were in no way breached.

The Trading Process

The establishment of Corn Exchanges was instrumental in the regularisation of the forward trading system. It was a natural extension of physical trading by sample, but due to its very nature variations to this practice were necessary: variations that were partly due to procedures and partly to case and efficiency, designed to foster operational advantage and equitability. In summary, the process may be divided into four constituent parts: negotiation, registration, formalisation and execution.

The process of negotiation was characterised by privacy rather than open publication. As delivery was infinitely variable, buyers and sellers first and foremost had to discover counterparts with corresponding schedules, whether this was at a time following harvest or by delivery ex stock. In the course of this process the two parties bargained over the price in a manner similar to the earliest of barter transactions until an indication of price was obtained. If only one delivery was consistent with the purchaser's needs, the contract may have been agreed upon on the spot. However, it was common practice for buyers to approach most, if not all, sellers in order to negotiate lower prices for identical produce upon the same or similar delivery date. The 'rounds' thus completed, the purchaser returned to the seller offering the most advantageous terms and the contract was settled. Importantly, sellers were precluded from re-negotiating should the purchaser return as offers were legally binding, providing the lapse in time was reasonable. Evidently, if the prospective purchaser returned days or weeks later, conditions could have changed dramatically, and original prices and delivery schedules were no longer applicable. But in ordinary circumstances, sellers were, to all intents and purposes, obliged to fulfil their promissory obligations, unless, of course, they had sold their produce in the interim period.

Resultant contracts were recorded by the exchange as to buyer, seller, description of goods, price, approximate or actual delivery date and became legally registered and thus enforceable. Formalisation was secured through the completion of pertinent contracts and not infrequently complemented by the independent lodging by each party to the transaction of a proportion of the contract value, also known as a deposit of good faith. Conceptually, it was the identical medium to the 'Denarius Dei' of the Middle Ages, acting as both a measure of good intent and security. In the event of default for any reason, the plaintiff was entitled to recompense from the recalcitrant party, irrespective of whether he was a buyer or seller, from the deposit impartially held in trust by the exchange. If need be the plaintiff instituted legal proceedings if this sum did not equate to the total loss incurred, whereas his contractual obligations were satisfied by a 'spot' or cash transaction.

In normal circumstances, however, contracts were executed in accordance with their terms. Upon the designated delivery date, the seller formally advised the buyer, who was then required to pay the residual amount of the contract and make arrangements for warehousing or delivery. The seller further advised the exchange of the completion of the transaction and requested the deposit which both he and his buyer had lodged in lieu of settlement, thus concluding the contract.

The Forward Pricing Structure

Under normal market conditions, the price of a commodity for spot or cash settlement differs from that for forward settlement. A combination of several evolutionary factors and the mechanism of forward trading itself directly influenced the manner in which forward prices were calculated. Increasingly, forward purchases were made ex-stock from warehouses owned by the merchants and farmers in advance of distribution. Therefore, many forward sales were agreed upon at a time when the goods in question were already tenderable. Consequently, at exchanges a price was given for both forward and immediate delivery; though commonly a difference existed between the two, with the forward price consistently above that for sale 'on the spot'. This differential was variable, but reflected the various expenses incurred by the farmers and sales merchants, which was sensitive to three essential elements.

The practice of good faith deposits to accompany each and every transaction necessitated the allocation of capital resources which might otherwise be deployed or, alternatively, credit arrangements had to be secured to perform this function. In either case, it implied loss through direct expenditure or unavailability of capital. Furthermore, immediate sale was accompanied with simultaneous full settlement, whilst on forward transactions payment was appropriately deferred. As cash sales did not require any security deposits, the additional cost and the length of deferral involved in forward transactions necessitated some form of financial consideration. As the deferral was viewed as a form of credit, the basis being the loss of interest if payment was made promptly, it became customary for the forward price to allow for the supplementary charges.

Insurance was by now regularly used in matters of transport, but progressive attitudes towards its more general advantages encouraged underwriting of several other risks, and losses due to fire, plague, flood or whatever were of major concern; particularly to the merchant who had contracted for forward delivery. The result was a growing incidence of insurance of stock and premises against such events, which relieved the vendors of their inherent dangers. Once again, the cost of the insurance policy was taken into consideration when forward sales were contracted, as cash sales avoided the need for such compensatory assurances.

In contrast to the direct delivery inherent in 'spot' dealing, many forward sales were, as outlined, supplied from stocks in sellers' warehouses, whereas this had hitherto been unnecessary. Consequently, storage costs were incurred by the sales merchants and farmers, who in turn transferred the expense pro rata onto purchasers of forward contracts.

The combination of these three costs inevitably resulted in a premium of price, known as a contango or forwardation, of forward sales over 'spot' prices. Furthermore, the more extended the period of deferred delivery, the greater the premium became, thus reflecting the time frame over which the expenditure had to be incurred. This pattern is a regular feature of forward contract pricing, although in extraordinary circumstances this may be reversed when demand for immediate physical delivery of any particular commodity rises above supply, forcing the 'spot' price above those involving deferred delivery despite the costs normally associated with forward contracts. This occurrence is termed 'backwardation'.

The Rise of Speculation

The rise of forward trading attracted interest and participation from various sources. One such group of participants was the speculators who, for the first time in many centuries, were freed of restrictions from buying and selling commodities for which they had no commercial use, uniquely for their own profit. From the analysis of information widely available through newspapers they endeavoured to predict fluctuations in prices over varying durations. Based upon their appraisals of market conditions they applied capital to their enterprises by either purchasing forward contracts in anticipation of rising prices or selling forward contracts in expectation of falling prices, which could each ultimately render a profit when the forward contract matured and they sold or bought on the spot market to cover their obligations.

Astute trading created potentially extraordinary returns which motivated even wider involvement. Their participation was assisted by the principle of trading by deposit payments. No longer were they obliged to find the full amount of the forward contract when it was struck. Rather, they relied upon the ability to off-set their positions in adequate measures which corresponded to their original forward contract obligations, and extracted the profit or loss at this stage. The attraction of fluctuating prices and unparalleled profit potential encouraged wider speculative sophistication and trading strategies, albeit the proportion of speculators remained relatively minor.

However, it would be very misleading to suggest that speculation was always successfully concluded. On the contrary, losses as significant as profits were realised, and speculation caused the financial ruin of many who, through inexperience, ignorance or misfortune, speculated in this way, Nonetheless, it was a growing feature of market activity, though its prominent emergence coincided, for good reason, with the establishment of futures trading which is examined in the following chapter.

Commodity Auctions

The second major trading innovation of the eighteenth century was the origination of auctions for many of the fashionable commodities which arrived from the East and the Americas. The arrival of commodity auctioning testified to a novel and radically different approach to marketing and illustrates the profound transformation of commercial philosophy. For the producer or seller of commodities, the organisation of events at which brisk competition inflates prices, particularly if supply was restricted or subject to control to some degree, was highly desirable. Hitherto many of the staple commodities were sold 'reasonable' or 'just prices', and distortions in price or racing inflation were countered by the government of the day, which imposed tariffs or subsidies and other fiscal and political measures to maintain prices at universally acceptable levels. The dissolution of this ideology was obviously of advantage to the producers, who, relieved of the fetters of governmental intervention, were eager to adopt marketing methods which accentuated their margins. Auctions, as such, were beckoning as a trading device.

The introduction of commodity auctions was, therefore, a natural development for many producers and merchants. Indeed, they became the traditional means of distribution for the soft commodities such as sugar, cocoa, and coffee, although the most noteworthy are the tea auctions, which are, due to their continued use, unique. For whereas their other 'soft' relatives have since progressed to futures markets (described in detail in the following chapter), the use of auctions has been retained as the primary method of marketing tea. To this day, tea auctions are regular events on international levels and for this reason much of the ensuing text chronicles the organisation and conduct of these auctions in particular. The general principles, however, may be safely applied equally to the trade in coffee, cocoa, sugar and rubber during the eighteenth and greater part of the nineteenth centuries.

The Rise and Effects of Tea Auctions

The popular demand for tea intensified progressively ever since its debut in the coffee houses of London in the seventeenth century. In response, the East India Company, recognising the significant commercial potential, exercised the right of monopoly granted under a charter in 1600, which permitted the organisation of auctions, and supplies previously secured through all other channels were terminated. Effectively, the market was subjected to legally sustainable price manipulation and both auctions and stock withholding ensured highly profitable ventures. By 1700, cargoes were regularly landed and introduced into the company's already established auction system. They were originally held in their warehouses, where candles were lit at the opening of the auction and concluded when one inch of the candle had melted away. At such time, the highest prevailing bid price was accepted, and the contract settled.

By the beginning of the eighteenth century some five hundred coffee houses sold tea, their supplies theoretically derived exclusively from the East India Company's inventories. In practice, however, this was not entirely true. For, despite laws which had previously prohibited imports from Dutch merchants, thus emphasising the monopoly the East India Company enjoyed, illegal imports were legion. The inflated price of tea, resulting from the enactment of the monopoly and the high level of excise duty, encouraged smuggling via vessels of foreign origin to satisfy the English penchant for tea which was rapidly becoming a social addiction. Syndicates of tea smugglers were endemic during the eighteenth century, collectively accounting for as much as sixty per cent of total bulk imports! Such were the benefits to the consumers of this contraband trade that merchants were held in great esteem, they established and serviced numerous retail outlets, and not infrequently newly-arrived supplies were stored in church vaults with the complete consent of the ministers concerned.

Smuggling persisted for several decades, to the dismay of the East India Company, which continually sought to enforce the terms of its charter. It was not until the passing of the Commutation Act in 1794 that this condition could be rectified. This provided for the duty imposed upon tea imports to be reduced drastically from 119% to just 12.5% although, in fairness, the motives for this were as much financial as they were political. The effect was to deflate the cost of legitimate merchandise significantly. In so doing, it rendered the colossal contraband trade all but defunct, and returned the East India Company's exclusive rights; but this was upon the proviso that it increased its imports considerably to correspond more accurately to the prevailing level of demand.

The proclamation thus restored the East India Company's monopoly of tea sales, and auctions were organised within the chambers of its own offices in Leadenhall Street in the City of London on an increasingly frequent basis to satisfy market demands. Continuing for almost fifty uninterrupted years, the East India Company became the single most important trader of tea in the world, although it was subjected to profound and bitter opposition from numerous entrepreneurs of the era.

Eventually, in 1832, an Act of Parliament was passed which revoked the monopoly charter and free trade was officially recognised for the first time. Some auctions were retained in the East India Company's offices until 1835, in order to release vast stocks of tea accumulated in the past onto the market gradually to prevent a total collapse in prices. Apart from this inventory clearance, auctions were transferred to the London Commercial Sale Room on 20th November 1934, which had been specifically built for commodity auctions in 1811.

For a period of several decades, auctions of the soft commodities were consolidated under one roof and their sales achieved unprecedented levels. It was not until the late nineteenth century that future markets had manifested themselves in England and gradually each of the soft commodities, save tea, witnessed the transition to the reputedly 'perfect' marketing system. Tea auctions continued in the pre-eminent London Sale Rooms for over a century, although the post World War II move to independence of many British colonies created bodies of trade associations in each of the producing countries which promoted domestic auctions, and their increasing influence over international sales diminished the standing of the London Sale Rooms. Thereafter, the London auctions were transferred to the Sir John Lyon House in the 1960's before coming to rest, for the meantime at least, in the premises of the London Chamber of Commerce from the end of 1990. Despite the relatively curtailed importance of London as the world's primary tea market, auctions collectively continue in an almost unaltered form; they remain prominent and regular international affairs.

Regulation and Organisation

The onus of organisation of sales facilities for many of the then contemporary commodities rested firmly on the shoulders of the producers and merchants, and certainly, in the evaluation of the commodities in question and the market in general, they determined the most favourable means of marketing. Following the revocation of the East India Company's monopoly, auctions were coordinated by associations composed of the above, which promoted the sale by issuing broadsheets, posters and advertisements and distributing circulars. The fixtures incorporated sales entered in lots which were presented in catalogues itemising each entry and supported by descriptions of their salient features. They were arranged by quality or origin rather than randomly to ensure a continuous, fluid affair. However, although there was qualitative categorisation, the quantity per lot varied enormously, albeit a standard chest size of some 1 cwt existed.

The frequency of auctions reflected the volume of the underlying trade; originally they were held by the East India Company at six monthly intervals. More regular shipments and unparalleled British consumption encouraged quarterly sales in March, June, September and December of consistently lengthening duration. By 1850, sales in the Mincing Lane Commercial Sale Rooms took place on a fortnightly basis; though, combined with other sales, auctions were conducted daily and consisted of up to fifty or sixty separate sales. Tea auctions expanded with consumer demand to the extent that lots were submitted every week-day. Nowadays, however, and as a consequence of the rise of producer countries' domestic auctions, the activity in London has since declined to a regular weekly event held on Mondays. Nonetheless, major auctions continue to be conducted throughout the week on an international level.

In contrast to the degree of trade regulation exercised by the government over other trading methods, auctions were subject to comparatively little formal control. Quality assurances were first addressed by Parliament in 1725, after continued reports of tea adulteration; for example, there were numerous accounts of connivance to comingle tea leaves with those from trees of domestic origin and, on rare occasions, even the addition of sheep dung to the blend! Statute naturally vehemently forbade this practice and imposed fines of one hundred pounds sterling on offenders and seized the adulterated produce into the bargain. Evidently, this activity was extremely difficult to suppress and successive Acts, in 1730-31 and 1766-67, increased the level of fines and provided for terms of imprisonment to inhibit the practice.

Routine internal regulation was, and remains, by way of codes of conduct rather than adherence to official rules which were largely unnecessary. As quality was subordinate to statute in the first instance and was appraised prior to each sale, the incidence of fraudulent dealings was minimised and became the subject of civil reparational actions. The importance of conduct was akin to that of the guild merchants of the Middle Ages insofar as reputation was essential to the well-being of individual and company alike. To this end, any dubious transactions were purged as any suspicion of malpractice potentially led to isolation. Reputations were bonds to the affairs of each individual and any perceived deterioration in credibility was potentially severely damaging. Accordingly, actions were rarely remedied internally, but were satisfied by civil prosecution and transgressors were prevented from any future dealings.

Parties and Roles

There were typically three groups of individuals present at negotiations. Brokers, both purchase and sales; independent officials; and frequently the brokers' customers or those with vested interest. The brokers acted on behalf of their principals, implementing the instructions provided in return for a commission. Sales brokers were strictly separated from purchasing brokers, and were prohibited from bidding. They were present nonetheless to survey market trends, advise sellers of price movements and recommend either acceptance or rejection of bids according to their perceptions and predictions.

Meanwhile, purchasing brokers were engaged by wholesalers or blenders to satisfy their inventory requirements at minimal cost. As numerous lots were entered, the ability to do this was exceptionally difficult, and was further compounded by the element of competition. However, despite the difficulties, the tea blenders and distributors developed an ingenious method of achieving their aims. The method is explained later in this chapter.

Whereas today there are relatively few companies engaged in blending and retail marketing, the eighteenth and nineteenth centuries were characterised by legions of middlemen and retailers each purveying different blends. During the early eighteenth century myriad individuals and companies bought at auction and sold on a retail level following their blending processes. As they bought in 'gross' lots of approximately 300-400 lbs, they were referred to as 'grossers' within the trade - a name which was later corrupted to 'grocers', currently applied to retailers of numerous household provisions.

On a wholesale level, however, the auctions were and are conducted by a director, who was selected by the selling brokers' association. His duties embraced the introduction of lots, and the conclusion of bargains, but his most specific vocation was the orchestration and continuation of a rhythm of bids. He was attended by two officials who recorded bids and their source and several clerks who registered contracts and initiated the pertinent sales documents. This system has remained virtually unaltered to this day.

But in contrast with forward trading, speculators have never been an intrinsic part of auctions, although there are no restrictions preventing this practice. However, that does not dismiss the presence of speculation altogether. In the 1840's Garraway's saw fervent speculative activity on a wholesale level as prices varied by as much as twenty-five per cent. Equally, there was considerable controversy over wholesale speculation in the 1920's. Nevertheless, the incidence of speculation is something of a rarity as the trade had devised an inventive method of absorbing oscillations in prices, and apart from intense shortages or extraordinary supply, the degree of variation generally tends to deter speculation.

The Auction System

The methods by which commodities are brought to auction and sold there has, similarly, altered very little since their inception and follows prescribed patterns. The owners of the tea estates commence proceedings by first contacting their sales broker and advising him of the precise details of the 'break' or lot (which may number as many as 120 standard tea chests of 1 cwt originally, though now 48kg) they wish to sell. Upon receipt of the consignment, the selling broker enters the break into an auction, to which a lot number is allocated and inserted in a catalogue produced by the selling brokers which itemises each of the lots. A sample of around two kilograms (5lbs) is extracted from each break and smaller samples are subsequently distributed to each of the buying brokers who act on behalf of the tea distributors. The dispersion of samples has been the responsibility of the Tea Clearing House since its formation in 1888. The samples are then introduced into tasting sessions held by each of the purchasing brokers on behalf of prospective buyers who assess their quality and, if they are found appropriate to the company's blend, a value is placed upon it.

Upon auction, the buying brokers, attended by their dealers, endeavour to procure the lots indicated by their clients until their counterparts refrain from further bidding or the price rises above that which their clients consider acceptable. Thereafter, depending on the tenor of the auction, they may be instructed to continue bidding or withdraw from proceedings and attempt to purchase other lots from different breaks as substitutes.

Bids were initially recorded in increments of one farthing (one quarter of one penny) ticks per pound, although today bids are recorded in ticks of one penny per kilogram. The bids do not constitute a contract, however, and undoubtedly the major advantage of auctions from a seller's perspective is the ability to remove the lot from the sale if it does not achieve the minimum acceptable sales value. Ordinarily, however, competitive bidding accomplishes satisfactory price levels and contracts are sealed. Thereafter, the Tea Clearing House registers the transaction, and the title documents are transferred to the purchaser, who is then notified of the precise location of the consignment. The documents provide authority to collect from the warehouse concerned; these are situated in London, Liverpool, Manchester, Bristol and Banbury. (Interestingly although London is the sole auction room in the United Kingdom, there are not and never have been centralised storage facilities). The collection and payment thus effected, the transaction is concluded.

Methods of Price Stabilisation

Not having the facility of forward trading to absorb radical price movements, the tea blenders have devised a unique method of stabilising relative values. Tea is known as a 'lead line' item. That is to say that it is ordinarily sold at extremely attractive prices by retailers as it is a staple product. Attractive prices also serve to induce consumers to purchase other groceries. Tea is also regarded as a 'known value' item, which demands a stability in retail prices. As the price of wholesale teas fluctuates, the blenders' profit margins are allowed either to increase or decrease, and only as a last resort are retail prices revised. The tea blenders are, therefore, acutely aware of prevailing prices and seek methods of protecting their profits. From the producer's perspective, concern is focused on minimum prices and failure to recover adequate returns results in the customary withdrawal of the lot and subsequent re-tendering.

The problems encountered by the tea blenders, by contrast, are far more acute. Ironically, the difficulties are overcome not through the means of trading, but are addressed by the experience and expertise of the blenders. Most teas available to consumers comprise leaves from several sources. They are, therefore, hybrid blends each containing perhaps twenty or thirty different teas which, combined, constitute a character peculiar to the distributor. The blender is responsible for the continuation of these distinctive qualities and may draw upon two or three hundred teas, each possessing varying individual attributes. He has, therefore, at his disposal almost infinite permutations of tea combinations which will preserve the blend.

When the price of a particular tea incorporated within the blend rises above a level which erodes profitability, the blender, using all his expertise, seeks teas with similar properties which may replace those which have become uneconomic. The effect is an abstention from bidding on the over-priced component which relieves general purchasing pressure and gradually reduces its value until it returns to a more conventional level. Only in extreme circumstances are severe shortages sufficiently serious to affect teas from various sources, with the consequence of exacting retail price increases. Under normal market conditions, however, blending is an entirely adequate means of stabilising profit margins and retail prices.

CHAPTER SIX

Forward into Futures

The nineteenth century continued very much as the eighteenth had dictated, characterised by rising population, greater dependence on industrial production, increasing contact with the New World, and unprecedented demand for basic raw materials and commodities. Individually, these elements created numerous commercial opportunities, whereas collectively they strained the tissues of industry and commerce. The consequence was the introduction and proliferation of a panoply of mechanical devices to improve productive efficiency and an equally vital reaction by commodity merchants and exchanges to the requirements of a more international trade and unremitting industrialism. But, if the institution of forward trading was barometric of the underlying economic climate during the eighteenth century, the establishment and formalisation of futures trading and markets during the nineteenth century was in every respect analogous, and addressed the very nature and extent of the prevailing problems.

Their inception was undoubtedly assisted by the invention of the electric telegraph in 1847, which revolutionised man's ability to communicate at hitherto impossible speeds and, thus, disseminate information and conduct negotiations almost immediately. In so doing, it eliminated the need to correspond by post or the necessity of physical transference of documents, instructions and information. Perhaps, however, the most beneficial consequence of telegraphic communications was the establishment of central market places which focused the interests of the commodity merchants onto major international fora, whereas previously they had practised at numerous regional centres.

Central markets improved the alliance between commodity producers and consumers; buyers and sellers were in closer contact with one another and, thus, able to monitor prices and supplies at the various provincial market places on a far more timely basis. The collective sensitivity of merchants to price fluctuations accelerated their response to localised shortage or abundance.

Accordingly, traders were far better positioned to identify niches in markets, and act decisively. In so doing, they were able to rectify prevailing conditions, and stabilise both prices and supply as a result. Effective communication between markets and amongst traders was paramount, and undoubtedly the invention of the telephone further reduced periods of market price aberrations and thus precipitated and encouraged market unity on a national and thereafter on a global scale.

The Transition to Commodity Futures Markets

The principal motive behind the establishment of futures trading largely corresponded to that of forward trading: the reduction or elimination of risk due to fluctuations in prices. It followed the extraordinary and explosive increase in demand for cotton during the nineteenth century which had replaced the pre-eminence of wool in the English economy. In contrast to the forward trading of grain, cotton was the subject of major trans-Atlantic traffic from the producing areas of the Southern States of America which, through the distance and length of journey involved, created perpetual price aberrations. Not uncommonly, vessels were away from their home ports for a year or more, and the voyage from the New World itself comprised two or more months at sea. The risks were therefore high due to the extended periods spent en route; for cotton merchants it resulted in extreme susceptibility to changes in domestic market conditions and highlighted a fundamental need for these risks to be reduced.

Originally, cotton merchants were issued with dock warrants when they entered their consignments into warehouses pending sale. As legal documents of ownership with descriptions of quantity and quality, each dock warrant was transferable upon disposal. Towards the end of the eighteenth century consignments were sold at England's premier and founding cotton market at Liverpool, not by auction as they had been in the past, but by the rather more orthodox method of stands with buyers approaching each of the vendors to inspect the various samples of merchandise they tendered. Upon successful negotiation, title was transferred in the manner described above, payment was effected and the contract was thus settled. However, the merchant importers who bought in the exchanges and markets of New Orleans and elsewhere in America were at considerable risk due to falling prices in periods between purchase and eventual sale at their home market.

This condition had long been the plague of the cotton sellers, and it was a problem which caused the financial ruination of those whose voyages proved consistently only marginally profitable or, worse still, unprofitable altogether. Based upon this fact, importers of cotton to England devised a technique which sought to mitigate the risks so that they could consolidate their profits. To an extent it was made possible by the first steamship crossing of the Atlantic by Samuel Cunard in 1840, which was inherently more rapid than the comparatively sluggish clipper vessels which had hitherto transported the cargo. The system was a simple one based upon time, both present and future. When merchants purchased cotton in America they loaded their consignments on board their vessels, but they simultaneously took samples and despatched them by steam ship. As the samples arrived in advance of the cargo they contracted to sell the cargo already en route 'on arrival'.

The drawback of the system was simply that precise or even approximate delivery dates were difficult to forecast, despite widespread knowledge of which cargoes were en route and whose sample were readily available for inspection. It was widely recognised that although the time span between purchase and sale was reduced thus reducing risk, the uncertainty of the duration in deferred delivery was far too long and erratic for it to be an acceptably efficient method of marketing. What in effect was required was a more accurate prediction of delivery so that greater reliance could be placed on the cargoes' arrival, in order to meet purchasers' inventory requirements more accurately.

In the event, it was a practice evolved by an unknown cotton trader who kept a constant vigil from Port Lynas in Anglesey, North Wales, of ships Liverpool bound. Through the identification of the vessel and the use of a fast courier to his Liverpool offices, he was able to refer to samples and information which had previously arrived by steamer. According to his observations, he was aware of what and how much cotton was due to arrive with a far more accurate idea of arrival. Armed with this unrivalled knowledge, he either bought or sold 'to arrive' in accordance with prevailing market conditions. Such was his success and profitability that the Liverpool Cotton Association, upon discovery of his intelligence methods instituted an official observatory and their sightings of vessels off Lynas was made simultaneously available to all concerned.

Arrivals contracts were thereafter exclusively traded in those cargoes whose vessels were in sight. The outcome was an emphatically broader market; it was a breakthrough in many respects which encouraged wider participation, particularly by speculators. The principles were sound, and the benefits were acknowledged by most of those who indulged in this practice, but many of the traditionally cautious merchants were unconvinced of the role of speculators and their ability to manipulate prices. Following a comparatively brief period of discussion, however, it was agreed that the speculative element to trading was conceptually beneficial as speculators assumed many of the risks the merchants sought to avoid; the advantages of their involvement were thus realised, but by this time the use of arrivals contracts had become accepted practice. In 1841, the Cotton Brokers' Association was formed and its codes of conduct were subsequently extended to embrace arrivals trading as an integral part of trade activity.

Meanwhile, in America, the Chicago Board of Trade was established. Despite the conflict in the Mid-West with native American tribes, Chicago developed into America's primary grain market. However, supplies were often delayed and erratic due to numerous encounters between the settlers and the natives. Contracts 'to arrive Chicago' and 'elevator receipts', much the same in conception to dock warrants, were used as evidence of title for deferred delivery, and a similar 'arrivals' trading method to that established in Liverpool was introduced.

Ironically, arrivals trading was not adopted by the American cotton merchants for more than two decades. This was due to the relative internal price stability afforded by greater consistency of supplies. Only during the American Civil War were supplies sufficiently sporadic to cause wide fluctuations in price and arrivals contracts were introduced on the New York Cotton Market during the 1860's.

Two further factors influenced changes to the principles of arrivals dealing, however. First was the relief of the Yankee blockade of the southern ports of America following its civil war. For several years the effectiveness of this blockade created extremely acute delivery problems; substantially reduced the volume of cotton exports which was the motive behind the blockade; and therefore caused ever rising prices. The lifting of the blockade permitted the revival of cotton exports which was predictably responsible for substantially lower prices at markets. For the cotton merchants the risks had become even more acute than before. For the relief of supply following the blockade brought prices sharply lower and they continued to fall for several months as cargoes were shipped at an unprecedented rate. It meant that in the interim period between its despatch and arrival at Liverpool, the market price was invariably considerably lower than that prevailing at the time of purchase. This was potentially ruinous for the cotton merchants concerned. It was obvious the 'arrivals' trading method was inadequate and a new device had to be found to reduce risks.

In the event, the solution was one of technology rather than technique. Indeed, it was the inauguration of the first trans-Atlantic telegraph cable in 1866 which solved many of the problems of selling cotton over wide distances and into a falling market. Speed of communication had become almost instantaneous as a result of this technology, which indirectly highlighted many of the inadequacies of the early arrivals contracts; but it also made an entirely new concept of trading possible.

John Rew was a Liverpool cotton merchant who devised a trading phenomenon we recognise today as 'hedging'. His theory was simple but effective. His hedging practice evolved around the simultaneous physical purchase of cotton in the United States and the sale, instituted by telegraph, of an arrivals contract sufficiently deferred for him to be completely confident of his being able to fulfil his obligations. At much the same time speculation in cotton prices was rife, but the principles of hedging did not discriminate between bona fide mill owners and speculators. His theory was based upon his ability to shift the risks onto other parties, which in so doing provided great flexibility. However, he did not always dispose of the physical cotton by means of the arrivals contract, but invariably relied upon the speculators to assume the risks whilst the consignment was in transit.

Upon its arrival he could sell his cargo at the prevailing market price and any loss he incurred between the time he sold the original arrivals contract and that at which he sold the physical merchandise was off-set by the profit which accrued on the arrivals contract when it matured. In this way he had 'hedged' his position so that regardless of short-term market movements, his profit was guaranteed at the rate his arrivals contract dictated. In so doing, he was able to separate his physical sales from his arrivals contracts if it were beneficial for him to do so, which in turn provided an unprecedented degree of price stability. Under no circumstance did he purchase cotton in the United States without instituting the appropriate arrivals hedge. Providing this was observed, his financial stability and profitability were unquestioned.

Notwithstanding the tremendous value of the new type of arrivals contract, development to some degree was entirely necessary if it were to become standard market practice. The Liverpool Cotton Brokers' Association formulated strict rules to govern the trade in speculative arrangements encouraged by their members. One major difficulty was presented by the enormous variety of terms of the original contracts as the merchants looked to hedge precise cargoes. It was a system which was simply becoming too cumbrous and time-consuming to be administered efficiently for the volume of transactions. Therefore, it was paramount that contracts were modified in someway. In the event, the breakthrough came with the introduction of 'general contracts' which were characterised by far more standardised terms. The first was quality. All arrivals contracts had to be 'basis middling - nothing below low middling' as it was impossible to inspect samples which were themselves still en route. It was a move which, similar to the Middle Ages' system of grading, simplified the trading procedure considerably.

The second term was time definition. In Liverpool, all subsequent arrivals contracts were subject 'to sail within one of two named months', and in New York, 'to sail in one named month'. These developments satisfied two criteria. First, the standardised terms enabled faster execution of hedging transactions as the contracts were more homogeneous; and second, their terms created a tremendous trading flexibility as the homogeneity they possessed made them more or less fungible with one another. In essence, the consistency of contracts permitted ease of entry and exit, which precipitated the formulation of increasingly complex trading strategies. Meanwhile, the improved communication facility reduced sellers' risks to a minimum as the delay in between their purchase and the institution of the appropriate hedge was virtually eliminated.

The origin of the term 'futures' remains unclear. The Chicago Board of Trade records the first 'futures' contract traded on the 13th October, 1865 and was based upon the contracts in operation on the Liverpool Cotton Exchange. Whether the term 'futures' was applied at this time, or added retrospectively at a later date is difficult to say. It is likely, however, the name 'futures' was not introduced until 1871, most likely in New York. By which time, the Mid-America Commodity Exchange had followed the lead of applying standardised terms to arrivals contracts in 1868 followed on the New York Cotton Exchange in 1870. Irrespective of the precise origin of the term, the principles of futures, founded in Liverpool some thirty-one years earlier, had become an intrinsic and invaluable tool in a broad spectrum of commodity trades. In the coming years, many commodities which had traditionally been sold at auction or by forward contract arrangements adopted the principles and practices of the infant futures contracts, but for very good reasons.

The Difference between Futures and Forward Trading

Not uncommonly, these two methods of trading are considered identical, but for the difference in name; while others mistakenly believe that futures trading evolved directly from forward trading. In fact, neither of these observations is true. There are fundamental differences between their operation, which are examined below. But whereas futures contracts were replacements for forward trading in certain instances, due to their superior qualities, they were never its descendants. Based upon these premises, it is a simple task to illustrate some of their basic differences.

i) Standardisation. Aside from the idiosyncratic arrivals contracts in the early stages, one of the most significant trading advantages of futures trading was the standardisation of contracts. Contemporary futures contracts incorporate qualitative as well as quantitative specifications in addition to specified trading months and a basis of delivery location. Standardisation is one of the most important aspects of trading, as the specifications have to correspond to a widely accepted standard. Certainly, acceptable specification was not always as straightforward as it might first appear. For instance, the London Corn Trade Association, in its endeavours to instigate futures contract facilities in 1887, had particular difficulty in introducing a satisfactory trading medium. Indeed, it was ten years before it found an acceptable contract standard. On the London Metal Exchange, by contrast, there were no 'official' contracts inititially. More by convention, however, Chile bars and Straits Tin became the standard grades for its copper and tin contracts. At the same time the period of the contract, 3 months, was standardised as this represented the approximate sailing times from both Santiago and Singapore to the U.K. ports.

The idea of universal acceptance of terms through standardisation is elemental. Forward trading, conversely, is subject to the individual negotiation of contracts according to precise and infinitely variable terms as to all aspects of price, quantity, quality, settlement date, delivery location and so forth. It is an inherently methodical and lengthy affair which is impossible to conduct on the scale of futures trading.

ii) Distribution. Forward contracts are essentially contracts of deferred delivery. Indeed, delivery at a predetermined point in time is fundamental to their constitution. Thereby, forward contracts may be regarded as distributive in operation and, in certain respects, substitutive of underlying 'spot' contracts. For if sufficient contracts had been arranged on a forward delivery basis, little use of the physical market is theoretically required. Futures contracts are, by contrast, almost exclusively non-distributive. That is to say that although provisions for delivery are incorporated in their terms, only a small percentage enter into the process of delivery. Moreover, positions can be opened and closed prior to the expiry of the contract, and cash differences representing profits and losses are posted to the accounts of those concerned. Seen in this light, futures contracts are complementary to those in the physical 'spot' market, where the task of distribution is performed.

iii) Risk Transfer. The principle of futures trading is the transfer of risk prevalent in volatile markets onto others willing to assume those risks with the intent of realising an acceptable financial gain. It varies quite markedly from the principles of forward trading. For although forward trading is concerned with the avoidance of risk, it undertakes this in an entirely different way. Indeed, it does not require any external participation to achieve this function. Risks, so far as forward trading is concerned, are therefore not subject to the principle of transference of risk prevalent in futures trading.

iv) Speculation. Whereas speculators participated in forward trading when it was re-established in the eighteenth century, their involvement, due to the burden of physical delivery, was by no means prolific. Indeed, their presence was but a minor proportion of those engaged in this type of trading. Futures markets, by contrast, are wholly dependent on speculators to accept the inherent risks so that the function of risk transfer can be performed. The introduction of standardised contracts was instrumental in the encouragement of such individuals as the transferability they preferred allowed unprecedented flexibility. Without the existence of speculators, who are afforded greater mention later in this chapter, the entire process of futures trading would be severely undermined.

v) Anonymity of Parties. Forward contracts incorporate the titles of the two parties as an intrinsic part or their composition. This is entirely necessary if delivery is to be effected in accordance with the contracts' terms. The use of brokers, and the large absence of physical delivery inherent in futures trading, however, eliminates the need for the two parties to be mutually familiar, Furthermore, the ability of either party to off-set his obligations, described in the section illustrating the characteristics of futures trading, means that counterparts to original trades are being 'replaced' (this is described in greater detail in the section dealing with Clearing Houses). Therefore, providing the brokers are aware of the identities of their clients, and contracts are correctly recorded and 'cleared' through an acceptable third party, the identification of contractual parties becomes redundant.

vi) Trading Pits. The concept behind the operation of both futures exchanges and their counterparts providing facilities for forward trading was the concentration of buyers and sellers. Early arrivals dealing was achieved in a manner quite similar to those in forward trading, typified by merchants circulating in their attempts to discover counterparts with whom to transact business. However, the volume of business at the Liverpool Cotton Exchange increased to a point where merchants, and brokers in particular, were allocated a specific area and runners relayed orders which had arrived by telegram to simplify the task at hand. The institution of the 'pit' or 'ring' resulted from the introduction of the general contracts as everyone present was able, to a greater or lesser extent, to fulfil orders which arrived. Traders therefore took up permanent places around the pit to form a circle and voiced their intentions either to buy or sell. Futures trading, thus, became a public affair at which all who were present were aware of the prevailing price and were extended equal opportunity to trade.

In certain instances, most notably in the metal trade, it became quite conventional to continue trading after the official market had closed. But in order for this to take place it had to be conducted outside in the street. Upon occasion, these gatherings became disorderly and were, as a matter of principle, returned to the exchange under unofficial terms. This type of trading, known as 'kerb dealing' remains to this day

vii) Open Outcry. Within these pits traders resorted to the traditional market practice of open outcry to publicise the orders they sought to execute, The private negotiations typical in arrivals trading were thus discarded, though this form of contracting remains a feature of forward trading. To its detriment was the intolerable level of noise which prevailed as traders attempted to make themselves heard. This condition was further compounded by the flow of trading instructions from messengers, particularly when direct telephone communications were established. In response, traders devised a form of tic-tac which provided visual representation of activity and price. It was invaluable for the efficient conveyance of information, and a useful side-effect was that it reduced the volume of noise. It survives to this day as a part of trading practice.

Futures Trading Characteristics

The institution of futures markets was acclaimed to be 'perfect' by many economists as buyers and sellers are brought together in an environment where everyone present is simultaneously aware of prevailing prices and is free to trade there. Combined with the principles of hedging, it is not difficult to rationalise why other commodity trades have adopted the procedures introduced by the cotton brokers of Liverpool. But examination of the features of futures trading reveals several additional aspects which endorse their popularity.

First, from 1880, margins were imposed upon all positions which represented a proportion, around ten per cent, of the contracts' values. Conceptually, they were similar to the deposits of good faith immanent in forward trading. Futures margins are, however, functions of risk, the more pronounced the risk becomes, the greater the margin becomes. To this end, margins are subject to variations according to movements of the underlying futures price. Therefore, loss making positions require the deposit not only of an initial margin when the original contract is taken, but a variation margin as well. Conversely, a position which moves favourably with the original position will see the repayment of the variation margin apart from that paid initially.

Second, the markets provided unparalleled flexibility through the ability to enter and exit positions by instituting opposite contracts to those originally taken. For example, the sale of one contract by A to B could be simply off-set should the trader wish to inhibit further losses or realise profits. In such circumstances, say the contract by A to sell, he could subsequently buy a contract identical in terms to his original contract from C. This would remove A from all contractual obligations, who would have his account debited or credited with the amount of his profit or loss and his margin would be returned in part or in full as this outcome dictated.

This facility is available due to the role performed by the Clearing House which interposes itself in each and every contract. To this end, the Clearing House becomes a buyer for every seller and a seller for every buyer; liquidation of positions is thus effected without the need for either delivery or the necessity of informing the original contract's counterparty. Traders, therefore, can initiate or terminate positions as underlying prices determine, with tremendous flexibility and in a manner which corresponds more precisely to their appraisal of market trends. The combination of these factors is noticeably absent from forward trading, which prescribes delivery. Naturally, traders can initiate opposite forward contracts, but it is invariably difficult to obtain exactly consistent terms. In any event, delivery has to be made and taken in accordance with the terms of the contract, which renders the process infinitely more burdensome.

Third, the nature of trade in the dimension of future time periods, together with the large avoidance of the need to accept or initiate delivery, enables traders to sell contracts which they neither have title to, nor the intention of obtaining, confident in the knowledge that they can purchase identical contracts prior to these contracts' expiry to eliminate any delivery obligations. The principle of selling contracts in advance of corresponding purchases is designed to yield profits in a falling market. It is known as 'going short' for reasons largely self evident. Conversely, the more orthodox procedure of buying prior to re-sale in times of rising prices is known as 'going long'.

Last, but by no means least, is the presence of display media which constantly up-date prevailing market prices, volumes and certain other trading statistics. Nowadays, technology permits the instantaneous and simultaneous dissemination of such information throughout the world. Effectively, market participants on opposite sides of the globe are equally able to monitor price trends and assume or terminate positions at extraordinary speed. Central markets have, therefore, become global fora, eliminating many of the drawbacks to physical location or time zone.

Options

Despite the attraction of futures as hedging instruments, they could not perform all risk management functions in the most efficient way. Not content with the disciplines of spot and futures trading, commodity brokers, producers and merchants looked to introduce a third dimension to cater for more specific needs. For instance, large scale commitments involving contract tenders introduced peculiar risks.

As there was never a guarantee that a tender would be accepted, those tendering were faced with a dilemma, should they hedge this exposure by using futures in anticipation of their tenders' acceptance and in so doing run the risk of an adverse market movement whilst their tender was rejected (thus losing on both accounts)?; or should they avoid the use of a futures hedge and hope that upon acceptance of their tenders the market for the commodities in question had not moved detrimentally in the interim, Patently, either course of action was inadequate. Not only did either solution not fully protect the tenderers against risk, each in effect invited risk. Therefore a solution had to be found.

In the event, it was a new type of instrument, options, which solved these problems. They were first introduced onto the London markets during the 1920's and have traded there continuously ever since. In reality, though, options were entirely new instruments which had not existed previously in

any tangible form, although admittedly they were derivations of methods of trading already in common use. So, what made options as attractive as they were claimed to be?

Options are contracts between two parties which incorporate rights for their purchasers either to buy from or sell to the sellers of the options, pre-determined quantities of a given commodity, at an agreed price, within a prescribed time frame. These rights may be exercised at any time prior to the options' expiry, but purchasers are under no obligation to do so if the price has moved adversely in the meantime. If the market price moved favourably with the terms of the option, the purchaser could then exercise the option, and the seller was obliged to perform his contractual obligations.

In effect, tenderers were able, through the use of options, to obtain a form of insurance; and for this insurance they paid a premium to the sellers which represented the buyers' entire financial liability. If the market moved contrary to the options' terms, they were simply allowed to expire and the premiums were written-off in much the same way as conventional commercial insurance policies. But, by definition, it implies a more favourable market price, at which the commodities involved in the tender may be acquired. Conversely, if the market moved to the benefit of the options, the return was unlimited and off-set the disadvantage of a less favourable market price should the tender be accepted.

Options, therefore, are perfect for hedging in circumstances where the commodities in question are not definitely required, but a provision against adverse market movements is necessary. Not surprisingly, options have become extremely popular instruments not just for this reason, but the feature of limited liability, coupled with unlimited profit potential, has also encouraged more widespread speculative use, which is outlined in more detail below. In any event, the use of options generally is increasing, rising to the point where today they are intrinsic to the commodity and commodity futures markets.

Speculation

At a comparatively early stage in arrivals dealing, it became obvious that growing speculative interest existed. Similarly, it was acknowledged that for the efficient execution of hedging there was a need for sufficient numbers of speculative buyers and sellers. Without them the task of risk transfer was extremely difficult to achieve, and in the absence of this function the undertaking of hedging was severely restricted. The assumption of risk, therefore, was considered and welcomed as the realm of the speculator.

Collectively, speculators provided the essential ingredient of liquidity in the market and their presence and utility should not be overlooked.

Speculators, however, needed little encouragement to participate as commodity prices constantly fluctuate in accordance with general market conditions, and the ability to go long or short to exploit rising or falling prices was and remains unique. Combined, these features provided unrivalled investment opportunities, far superior in many respects to other investment media. The introduction of general contracts was another significant step forward for speculators, as the facility to enter and exit markets through the uniformity of the trading instrument provided unprecedented flexibility. However, speculation did not always yield positive results and many were to suffer embarrassing financial loss.

The reason for the high degree of risk involved is due in part to the volatility of prices over even the briefest of periods. But the risks are accentuated through what is known as 'gearing' which is a consequence of trading on margins. In normal circumstances, margins represent approximately ten per cent of the total contract value. Therefore, if the total value of one contract is one thousand pounds, the speculator, irrespective of whether he first buys or sells, is required to deposit a margin of just one hundred pounds. If the price of that commodity alters to the tune of ten per cent, a none too uncommon move, the profit or loss of this movement is tantamount to one hundred per cent of the capital employed. Seen in this light, it is readily apparent that, through the leverage accorded by way of margins, risks are far greater than those in alternative investments. This was, however, not altogether a deterrent. In typical fashion, the participation of many speculators was re-appraised which in turn led to a modification of approach. Gradually, syndicates of speculators were formed to limit the degree of personal risk, but in a manner which retained the potential of substantial profit. Ironically, one of the merchants' earliest fears, that of artificial price manipulation by speculators, was realised.

Most syndicates were completely rational in their approach and operated with the sole intention of acceptable financial returns. Upon a few occasions, however, syndicates surpassed the general bounds of their utility and some have attempted to corner markets through concerted manipulation. One such syndicate, spearheaded by a Frenchman, Pierre Secretan, endeavoured to control the copper market in the late nineteenth century, while an equally noteworthy attempt by the Texan Nelson 'Bunker' Hunt at the beginning of the 1980's in the silver market provides a more recent example. On both occasions the market returned to normal, albeit for different reasons, but the outcome was identical. As the middlemen of the Middle Ages had always claimed, the markets were too profound in material interest to be subjected to prolonged periods of artificial prices.

The incentive of potentially enormous speculative profits generated a tremendous sophistication in trading techniques. Not only were the merchants developing intricate hedging strategies, but speculators were also active in investigating different ways to trade, whilst simultaneously attempting to minimise the inherent risks. Clearly, futures trading was rapidly becoming a specialist discipline, which in turn gradually discouraged the involvement of many who were unable to keep pace with developments. Upon the introduction and proliferation of options, many speculators diverted their interests to this medium. Through options many of their speculative objectives could be achieved, but without the corresponding liabilities inherent in direct futures trading. But apart from those who indulged in options, many speculators withdrew from trading, citing four separate elements.

First, the risks, even in relation to potential rewards, were considered to be inordinately high; second, in the light of increasing sophistication, the amount of capital required to trade effectively was becoming excessive; third, the markets presented considerable difficulties for those with insufficient time to appraise trends and information, or those who possessed either inadequate experience or expertise; and fourth, the presence of unlimited liability present in futures trading compounded the inherent risks.

However, despite these problems, the speculative element to futures trading continued, but for it to be properly accommodated a new approach had to be found. Therefore, more recently, investments in the form of commodity funds were devised and introduced by commodity brokers and specialist investment managers. They feature liability limited to the investors' initial capital outlay; the minimum investment was reduced from a traditionally high figure to but a few thousand pounds, and professional managers were charged with the responsibilities of trading. Their success was virtually immediate, Almost every investment criterion seen as a barrier was satisfied and the opportunity for the broader investing public to diversify portfolios into commodity futures markets had become a reality.

Clearing Houses

The institution of clearing houses can be traced back to the Champagne Fairs of the Middle Ages, but although they disappeared for centuries following the fairs' abandonment of commercial activities, clearing houses re-appeared in the nineteenth century in a form almost identical in format to that of their forerunners. Indeed, apart from technological advances even their operation has been modified very little since.

Under the system of arrivals contracts in Liverpool, runners and messengers were employed by each firm to distribute contracts in accordance with those agreed on the trading floor. Independent records were kept by each party and terms were verified to ensure accuracy. But following the introduction of general arrivals contracts which were more homogeneous and therefore more flexible, the settlement process encountered a number of difficulties, Initially, clerks frequented the offices of the various brokers so that all expired contracts could be settled in cash.

Two major drawbacks existed, however. The first was the incidence of attack upon, and the theft from, the clerks who were responsible for the collection of debts. The second was unfounded delays in payment and, on occasion, default by clients. The volume of transactions following the use of general contracts rendered this archaic method obsolete. It was replaced with a system designed and implemented by the brokers' bankers. Each day representatives from the banks met to calculate the extent of indebtedness each member had to its counterparts, whereupon only the appropriate balances were transferred in paper transactions without the physical movement of cash. Although this solved many of the problems of robbery, it did not prevent default. The integrity of the market was founded upon that of its members and patrons. So, if either proved untrustworthy, the standing of the market was completely undermined; the result of which would be a complete collapse of confidence and participation.

Accordingly, much stricter controls had to be introduced which ensured the market's integrity and therefore its continued well-being. So, in 1874, the Cotton Brokers' Association established its own Clearing House for settlement upon similar lines to the banking clearing system. This was re-organised in 1878 under the name of the Cotton Brokers' Bank Ltd, which collected cheques from debtors and issued credits as appropriate. It differed from its predecessor insofar as it demanded that members paid into and received monies from a fund common to all involved. In so doing, it eliminated duplication of inter-member payments, but more importantly, transactions were being more closely monitored. From 1980, a settlement price was published each day to which all outstanding positions were compared. In this way, the Clearing House called for variation margin from those whose positions were in debt and returned margin to those whose positions were moving favourably. Accordingly, the risk of default was minimised as positions were being 'marked to market' far more regularly, and settlement of positions was simplified to create far greater efficiency.

On the 22nd February 1888, the London Produce Clearing House (L.P.C.H.) was organised to perform similar functions to those of the Cotton Brokers' Clearing House. In the 1950's it was absorbed into the United Dominions Trust Ltd and re-named the International Commodities Clearing House (I.C.C.H.) in 1964. Ironically, the ownership turned full circle in 1981 when it was, purchased by Britain's five major commercial banks which each retain twenty per cent of the shareholding.

Clearing Houses became an intrinsic part of the futures markets' constitution, with duties and responsibilities invaluable to the efficient conduct of trade. The first is the registration of all contracts concluded and the duty to reconcile every buyer with a seller and vice versa to ensure contractual accuracy. Second, based upon those contracts recorded, it monitors all open positions and imposes initial or variation margin as appropriate and repays similar amounts for those whose open contracts are due a part of their variation margin commitments or whose positions have been off-set. The Clearing House also imposes a small levy on every transaction it clears, which is used in part to guarantee the fulfilment of each contract. In the event of contractual default, the clearing house buys or sells on the open market as the abandonment of obligations dictates and in so doing arranges a substitute for the defaulter's contract by a system known as 'novation'. Any difference between the price at which the replacement contract was struck and that of the original is covered under the terms of the guarantee. For this reason, there has never been a case whereby a commodity futures contract has not been fulfilled according to its original terms.

Regulations

In Britain regulation of the futures markets and their members is subject principally to internal organisation. Under government legislation introduced concurrently with the 'Big Bang' in 1987 various Self-Regulatory Organisations (SRO's) were organised under the auspices of the Securities and Investments Board (SIB). So far as the futures markets are concerned the SRO was the Association of Futures Brokers and Dealers (A.F.B.D.). The introduction of a self-regulatory body was partly at the instigation of the futures industry itself which demanded a far greater role in the regulation of the markets' members. But it was also consistent with the recommendations of Professor Gower, who was commissioned by the government in 1981 and again in 1983, following a number of incidents which were damaging to the integrity and reputation of the London markets and members alike. His brief was simply to investigate ways in which the futures markets could best be regulated.

Since April 1991, the A.F.B.D. has merged with the Securities Association (T.S.A.) to form a much more simple and harmonious regulatory structure. The authority now responsible for the regulation of both the futures markets and securities trading is the Securities and Futures Authority (S.F.A.). However, despite the change in name and wider brief, its principal responsibilities with regards to the commodity futures markets remain unaltered. Though it is not wholly necessary for the purposes of this book to examine the intricacies of regulations, it is appropriate to mention the main areas of business over which the S.F.A. has jurisdiction. They are:—

i) Codes of conduct;
ii) Standards of reporting and accounting;
iii) Segregation of clients' funds from those of the broker;
iv) Investigation of complaints;
v) Compensation for non-trading related losses.

Those under the auspices of the Authority who fail to observe any of the Codes or Rules are answerable to the S.F.A. in the first instance. They are subject to either fines, for minor offences; or upon occasion, and should the offence be of sufficient gravity, the company or individual may be prevented from continuing business by the Authority and may well be referred to the Department of Trade for criminal prosecution. For although the S.F.A. has the power to punish and control companies and individuals for breaches in codes of conduct or rules, it is not empowered to institute legal proceedings.

In this way, those wishing to conduct business are very closely examined to ensure that the company and its officer are 'fit and proper'. That is to say that the company must be financially sound and meet minimum capital requirements; whereas those who are engaged by the recognised companies have to be honest and competent to undertake business on behalf of customers. The intention is to avoid any possible mis- or mal-practice and to safeguard the interests of clients at all costs.

The S.F.A. is, however, only concerned with the conduct of those it regulates and their relationship with their clients. Concurrently, each exchange upon which commodity futures are traded has rules and regulations in respect of conduct on the exchange between the members themselves. Floor officials are present on each exchange and at each pit where different contracts are traded. Their duties are to monitor conduct to ensure gentlemanly behaviour, settle minor disputes and to enforce market regulations. Any serious breaches are reported to the Secretary of each exchange for investigation. If mis-conduct is proven, the individual and, perhaps even on occasion, the member, may be fined; or if the breach was particularly serious, suspension or expulsion may result.

In summary, it means that every facet of practitioners' activities, whether between one another or with clients, is subject to a high degree of regulation. Members, in order to ensure full observation of all such regulatory requirements, now have Compliance Officers dedicated to this task. But although the companies themselves may complain of an inordinate number of rules, they are wholly necessary to ensure complete customer confidence and therefore, a successful exchange.

Future Developments

The phenomenon of hedging and the use of futures in the Cotton trade was a major development in the trade of commodities of all descriptions and origins. Gradually, many commodities traded by other more traditional methods, such as forward contracts or auction, made the transition to Futures. Today, commodities traded on London's futures markets embrace metals, agricultural products such as wheat, barley and potatoes; oil; 'soft' commodities such as cocoa, coffee and sugar; and rubber. But at the same time, the principles of futures trading have been applied to an entirely new sector - financial instruments. Money is perhaps the ultimate commodity, so it is also worthy of mention here. For trading in futures on currencies, interest rates, government debt instruments and the stock market are each highly traded contracts on the London International Financial Futures Exchange, which was established in September 1982. This introduced a new and entirely different market in futures and the phenomenon of futures moved on yet another step. But it is unlikely that the trade in futures will end here. Indeed, there are already developments which will alter the complexion of trading in the foreseeable future.

New 'commodities', whether abstract or traditional, may be introduced at any time, for the principles of futures can be applied to an unlimited variety of trades. But more noteworthy changes are likely to be the consequence of technology rather than technique. Through the remarkable sophistication of computers and satellite communications, futures markets are becoming global affairs rather than international. That is to say that markets are rapidly becoming 24-hour affairs to embrace ever-increasing global participation. This has largely resulted from the advent of computer exchanges which do not observe natural human frailty and, therefore, the normal boundaries of market hours. Through the use of computer terminals in members' offices linked to the mainframe computer located in the exchange, bids, and offers can be posted with the minimum of delay, and with commendable efficiency.

However, although trading of this type is presently complementary to regular exchange hours and the open outcry system, the tide towards greater computerisation is advancing and many traditionalists are opposed to the devotion to computers and the abandonment of open outcry. For physical contact between market participants has been a hallmark of the markets' success, but by eliminating direct human presence the markets become 'ghost like' and cold. The fear is that although the functions of markets may be perpetuated by using computers, the spirit will disappear, whether computer markets will completely replace open outcry will depend upon whether economics prevail over tradition. But global markets absorb and invite greater competition, so the necessities of economics will become a pre-requisite for survival. In any event, although the futures markets themselves look set to continue to go from strength to strength, the longer-term outlook for preserving open outcry is rather more nebulous.

Commodity Swaps

Another, more recent, form of hedging has been introduced to the trade in commodities following that in the financial markets. Although 'swaps' in currencies and interest rates have existed since the early 1970's, equivalent swap contracts have been traded on commodities only since the latter part of the 1980's. In essence, a 'swap' is an exchange of obligation, typically referring to that between a fixed price and that of a variable nature. They were adapted from financial swaps, but found immediate acceptance in commodity based transactions in view of the traditionally high level of commodity price volatility. Indeed, the average price volatility over time of several commodities can be double or more that of financial products. This inevitably introduces an element of risk for both producers and consumers of commodities which needs to be reduced, if not eliminated. Futures markets provide a partial solution, but have limitations: limited time horizons, standard contract terms and limited variety. So, an alternative and additional hedging medium was welcome.

Swaps, therefore, are hedging arrangements, used to minimise risk, but differ from traditional futures contracts in that no delivery is made. They are also serial contracts in that an 'exchange' takes place at variable intervals dependent upon the prevailing price throughout the life of the swap. For example, an exchange may take place each month on a specified date for, perhaps, six consecutive months. The exchange is in effect a settlement based upon the difference of a 'fixed' price agreed at the time of contracting and the variable or 'floating' price either when exchange is due to take place or an average of the floating prices for the period concerned. But, in either case the exchange does not involve the total amount of the contract. What it does represent is the difference in price of the fixed and floating components multiplied by the nominal quantity of the commodity in question. The contract is thus settled in cash and involves no physical movement of the underlying commodity. The swap can, therefore, be considered to be a mechanism purely to 'fix' the price of a commodity over an agreed period of time.

Concurrent with the swap are the separate spot or physical commodity transactions which continue to perform the distribution function. The swap, meanwhile, offsets price volatility For, in effect, buyers continue to procure physical produce from sellers in the ,'spot' market at the prevailing price, but either pay or receive cash settlements which equate to and compensate for short-term movements through the swap, but with perhaps entirely different counterparts. For instance, the buyer of the swap, normally a consumer, would continue to procure supplies 'spot' and should the price be above the price fixed he would receive, separately from his swap counterpart, the difference in price relating to the quantity concerned, Conversely, should the price -'spot' be below that of the fixed element of the swap, he would pay the difference to the swap counterpart. Accordingly, the profit on the swap offsets a loss on the spot market, while a loss on the swap offsets any benefit received from buying spot. In this way the price is assured at the level of the swap fix for the duration of the swap agreement.

The benefit to the producer offering a fixed price for the swap is the assurance of profitability of production over time, so that therefore, he needs to contend with supply variances only. Consumers in the meantime are able to secure a fixed price, which in so doing eliminates price volatility risk. Ipso facto, suppliers lock in receipts over time while simultaneously assuring themselves an acceptable profit margin, whereas consumers lock in payment flows and can build into budgets and cost analyses actual costs for certain raw materials over a specified period of time.

One further attraction of swaps is that the range of products which may be traded in this way is potentially much wider than those commodities traded on a futures exchange. Whereas every commodity futures contract may be incorporated into a swap, any commodity which can rely upon a fixed accurate reference price may, theoretically, be swapped. Futures prices can provide an acceptable reference price for many commodities, but are not available upon many derivatives of the commodities concerned. There are also a number of commodities which do not benefit from a liquid futures contract, but which can be swapped if a suitable reference price can be agreed upon. That said, the majority of swaps are run in conjunction with futures contracts as much position hedging is accomplished through the use of several calendar-serial futures contracts.

For these reasons, swaps are particularly valuable in the oil market, but have also found wide scope in the metals markets. Traditional 'soft' commodities, such as coffee, cocoa and sugar, are also 'swappable', but the contracts' durations are invariably much shorter due to crop cycles and external supply-side variances.

A swap is, therefore, a hedging instrument, but is a hybrid of several other instruments. It is not a futures contract, as it is not traded on any exchange; it does not incorporate standard terms; it does not allow anonymity; and is not guaranteed by any clearing authority.

Meanwhile, although the aforementioned suggests the swap resembles a forward contract, it is not distributive which in itself is an intrinsic part of a forward arrangement. However, swaps are more closely allied to forward contracts in that terms are negotiable, counterparties are mutually familiar with one another, and there is no opportunity for offset in the way in which futures contracts allow. Rather, a swap is valid for the contract's duration. A swap can be matched by a similar or identical swap of reverse terms, but the original swap will remain intact until the contract's expiration,

Though a recent innovation, commodity swaps have already received wide support from a multitude or industries throughout the world. They are complementary to more traditional forms of trading and hedging, but retain unique characteristics. For these reasons, they add a further trading dimension to those already in existence and are hailed by many as displaying perhaps the greatest growth potential in commodity trade over the next decade.

Summary and Conclusion

Ever since there has been a trade in commodities, markets have proven to be highly efficient conduits of activity. They are, in many ways, the organs of trade through which the blood of commercial prosperity flows. Time and again they have been shown to be indispensable to the well-being of trade and have grown or developed to ensure the survival and progress of trade. Apart from the austere period of the Dark Ages, progress has been undeniable and continuous. For markets and their practices have responded to changes in economic patterns and political stimuli alike. They have performed the task of distribution in exemplary fashion and have in so doing reduced regional inequalities and price volatility to a minimum.

Irrespective of the image, the mechanics of commodity markets are unquestionably designed for the good of all who consume, produce or trade in commodities. However, for this function to be perpetuated and improved, further developments are likely. How and when they might appear is anybody's guess, but having witnessed almost constant development over two millennia, it is at this stage impossible to believe that future embellishments will not be forthcoming.

Epilogue

A good decade has passed since the original edition of 'From Forum to Futures' was published and the expectation that more developments would take place has held true. Indeed, two major changes have occurred in particular, one almost foreseeable, the other almost ironic in its nature. The former revolves around automation, the latter concerns the consolidation and re-privatisation of exchanges. In a way, they are closely linked.

The potential automation of exchanges was already a bone of contention. No one doubted that technology would have an impact on the way in which commodities were traded in the UK and globally beyond, the question was moreover to what extent would it pervade centuries old practices.

Major improvements in computerised trading platforms followed to the point that the traditional open-outcry markets could scarcely compete. While this originated mainly in the financial derivatives markets, the effects were certainly felt in the commodities markets also. The so-called 'tech boom' at the end of the 1990's brought with it a whole new generation of exchanges - 'B2B' or 'business to business' markets designed to bring buyers and sellers of a wide range of commodities together over internet facilitated networks. It was a revolutionary idea - and held great promise, in principle at least.

The idea was to bring into an open, transparent forum the trading of some quite exotic as well as well-established physically traded commodities. The ability to link traders, consumers and producers around the world, it was postulated, would lead to improved price discovery, more efficient markets and enhanced trading possibilities.

But then, as the sages of the day concurred, what if the cash commodities markets could be linked with the derivatives exchanges to provide a two-dimensional trading platform? Wouldn't that be of even greater benefit? And if so, why not try to embrace the customised over-the-counter (OTC) market in various derivative structures such as swaps to produce a universal, all encompassing trading facility? Would that not be the ultimate in market places?

As it happened, huge amounts of money were invested in the UK (as well as the

Epilogue

US, Europe and the Far East) to build such a platforms. Commodities ranging from the well-established trade in coffee, cocoa, and sugar to the esoteric in chemicals, minerals, even weather, came into focus. But the bursting of the tech bubble meant that the money ran out for many before the dream could be realised. Most went bust. Others scaled-back; some merged. But the footprint remained and the dream never completely ended.

There is little of this legacy still to be seen, however. Most of the B2Bs have since disappeared although the impact of the technological revolution is visible. Open out-cry trading in a number of commodity derivatives is now a thing of the past; trading is fully automated while others are relying increasingly on ever greater technological support. This seems certain to continue, even though the reappearance of B2B exchanges is less clear.

The second major development seems in some ways to pay heed to history and times when markets were privately owned and operated as businesses in their own right. The demutualisation of exchanges from member-owned utilities to profit-motivated commercial enterprises saw a wholesale transformation of the way many exchanges were operated. In part, this was propelled by changes to the regulatory environment in which effective monopolies were being removed and partly because the competition being introduced from fledgling exchanges, B2Bs amongst them, meant that many exchanges had to become more efficient and focused. Privatisation was seen as the best way to improve competitiveness and to unlock the commercial values and potential held for so long mutually in trust.

This in turn led to the consolidation of exchanges, markets and systems as economic demands prevailed. In the UK, there have been two quite notable developments where commodities are concerned. The first, is the 'merger' of the London Commodity Exchange (LCE) with the London International Financial Futures and Options Exchange (LIFFE). The second, is that of the takeover of the International Petroleum Exchange (IPE) in London by a 'tech-boom' newcomer, the InterContinental Exchange (ICE) based in the US.

In some ways there is irony in both of these cases. The first is the effective take-over of a long established commodity derivatives' exchange by one of its off-spring, namely a financial derivatives exchange. While in the second case, it was one of the few successful B2B-type platforms that survived and prospered enough to takeover a well-established commodity derivatives exchange. Many would have guessed the inverse would have prevailed.

Epilogue

So, the story continues. Technology continues to dictate the direction and pace of change and the quest for efficiency and longevity remains. There is little reason to think that this is about to change.

Bilbliography

History of Rome. Michael Grant 1978 (Weidenfeld & Nicolson)

A History of the Roman People. Fritz Heiehelheim, Cedric Yee, Allen Ward 1984 (Prentice Hall)

The Decline of the Ancient World. A.H.M. Jones 1975 (Longman)

The Ancient Economy. M.I. Finley 1985 (Chatto & Windus)

A History of the Ancient World. Chester Start 1974 (Oxford University Press)

A History of Europe 911-1198. Z.N. Brooke (Barnes & Noble)

An Economic Development of Medieval Europe. R.-H. Banner 1977 (Thames & Hudson)

The Medieval English Economy 1150-1500. J.L. Bolton 1980 (J.M. Dent & Sons)

The Economic History of England Volumes I-III. E. Lipson 1966/71 (Adam & Charles Black)

The Cambridge Economic History of Europe. 1989 (Cambridge University Press)

The Making of English Towns. David Lloyd 1984 (Victor Gollancz Ltd)

The Economy of Later Renaissance Europe 1460-1600. Harry Miskimin 1975 (Cambridge University Press)

Sixteenth Century England. Joyce Youings 1984 (Penguin Books Ltd)

The Collins Guide to Markets and Fairs of Great Britain. Janice Anderson 1988 (Collins)

The Village in History. Graham Nicholson & June Fawcett 1988 (Weidenfeld & Nicolson)

The English Town. Mark Girouard 1990 (Yale University Press)

The City of London: a financial and commercial history. R. Gibson-Jarvie 1979 (Woodhead-Faulkner)

Tea For the British. Denys Forrest 1973 (Chatto & Windus)

Index

Agents 23, 60-61
Alfred the Great 14, 18, 19
Arrivals Contracts 82-86, 88, 94
Assize, the system of 23, 31, 48
Association of Futures Brokers and Dealers, the 95-96
Auctions 73-79, 81, 85, 97

Backwardation 72
Banking 37
Bartering 1, 7, 16, 70
BlackDeath, the 31, 34
Black Markets, the 9, 10, 12
Blenders, Blending 73, 79
Bounties 61-62
Bracton, Thomas 33
Brokers 41, 42, 63, 77-78, 87, 90, 93-94
Burton, the Abbot of 34

Cartels 58
Carters 28, 51, 59
Champagne Fairs, the 37-38, 93
Charles the Bold 18, 31
Charters 18, 29, 31, 32, 33, 35, 36, 41, 43, 55, 73-75
Cheaps, Cheapmen, Cheaping 40
Chicago Board of Trade, the 83, 85
Church, the 15, 18, 20-22, 23, 24, 32, 35, 74
Clearing Houses and System 37, 38, 78, 87, 89, 93-96, 100

Codes of Conduct 22, 28, 69, 76, 83, 96-97
Coffee Houses 62-64, 73-74
Coinage 7, 9
Commodity Funds 93
Commodity Swaps 98-100
Common Crier, the 36
Computer Exchanges 97-98
Contango or Forwardation 72
Com Exchanges 51-52, 69
Corporations 55
Cotton Brokers' Bank Ltd, the 96
Couriers 59-60, 82
Courts 6, 8, 22, 43, 44-45
Cunard, Samuel 83

Deferred Delivery, Contracts of 11, 53, 82-83, 86
Denarius Dei 53, 70
Deposits 53, 70-72, 89
Doomsday Book, the 31
Duties 61-62, 66, 74

East India Company, the 73-76
Edgar, King 23-48
Edward I 29
Edward III 33
Edward VI 55
Elizabeth I 55, 63
Embargoes 29, 33, 62
Emporium, the 4, 5, 15, 17
Engrossers 47, 57-58

Index

Factors 60, 69
Fairs 29, 34, 35-40, 42, 44, 46, 50,96
Fines 8, 10, 12, 45, 47, 48, 53, 76, 96-97
Forestallers, Forestalling 47, 50, 52-58, 62
Forum, the 4, 5, 15
Forwardation, see Contango
Forward Contracts, Trading 11, 12, 53, 54, 67-72, 77, 79-81, 85-89, 97, 100
Futures Contracts, Trading 73, 75, 80-100

Gearing 92
General Contracts 85, 88, 92, 94
Gower, Professor 96
Grossers, Grocers 77
Guildhalls 48, 51
Guilds 27, 28, 32, 40, 41-45, 47, 48, 49, 51, 54-56, 76

Hedging 84-85, 90-91, 93, 97-100
Hoarding 12, 57
Hunt, Nelson 'Bunker' 92

Inns 33, 62-64
Insurance 60, 71, 91
International Commodities Clearing House Ltd, the 95

Just Prices 41, 45-47, 52, 58, 73

Kerb Dealing 88

Laissez-Faire Economics 66
Lex Mercatoria, Law Merchant 23, 44-45
Licences 10, 15, 29, 30, 32, 34, 39, 41, 42, 45, 54-55, 69
Liverpool Cotton Exchange, the 81, 88
London Chamber of Commerce, the 75
London Commercial Sale Rooms, the 75-76
London Corn Trade Association, the 86
London International Financial Futures Exchange, the 97
London Metal Exchange, the 86
London Produce Clearing House, the 95
Lyon, Sir John, House 75

Manipulation 12, 41, 46, 47, 54-55, 57, 59, 83, 92
Margins 89, 92, 94-95
Market Crosses 21, 34, 45, 48, 51
Market Halls 38, 51
Market Overt, principle of 46-47
Marts 19, 35
Middlemen 41, 47, 54-58, 61
Monasteries 22
Mongers 41

Novation, principle of 95
Nundinae 5

Open Outcry 36, 88, 98

Index

Options 91-91, 93

Pecunia 7
Pedlars 15, 23, 40
Police, Policing 6, 8, 22, 44
Port Lynas 82
Price Fluctuations, Volatility 3, 4, 7, 11, 62, 66, 67-68, 72, 77-79, 80-81, 83, 92, 98-99
Price Guarantees 7

Quality Controls 9, 23, 43, 48, 56, 76, 85-86

Rations 7
Regraters 47, 57-58
Regulation 6, 9, 10, 19, 22, 23, 31, 43, 45, 55, 69, 75-76, 95-97
Rew, John 84
Richard I 48
Royal Exchange, the 63

Samples, Sales by 4, 51, 53, 69, 78, 81-82, 85
Secretan, Pierre 92
Securities and Futures Authority, the 96
Securities and Investments Board, the 95
Smith, Adam 62
Speculators, Speculation 7, 11, 12, 60, 68, 72, 82-84, 91-93
Standardisation 9, 23, 31, 38, 48, 59, 85-87, 98, 100

Staple, System and Ports 29, 30, 34, 39, 41, 42, 44, 53
Steamships 82
Subsidies 7, 30, 62, 66, 73
Syndicates 92

Tariffs 10, 61, 73
Telegraph, the 80, 84, 88
Telephones 81, 88
Tenders 90-91
Tic-tac 88
Tolls and Taxes 3, 7, 8, 10, 11, 16, 19, 24, 27, 29, 30, 32, 35, 36, 38, 42, 43, 45, 48, 52-54, 67
Tooms, Tombland 14
Trading Rings and Pits 63, 87-88, 97
Transport 3, 4, 5, 13, 27, 28, 30, 37, 56, 82

Weights and Measures 9, 23, 38, 48
Weyhill Fair, the 37
Wiks 24, 25, 32, 40
William the Conqueror 19, 29
Witnesses 16
Woolmen, Wool Staplers 42, 55-57